M000012439

Louisiana Legal Research

CAROLINA ACADEMIC PRESS
LEGAL RESEARCH SERIES

Suzanne E. Rowe, Series Editor

§

Arizona, Second Edition — Tamara S. Herrera

Arkansas — Coleen M. Barger

California, Second Edition — Hether C. Macfarlane, Aimee Dudovitz
& Suzanne E. Rowe

Colorado — Robert Michael Linz

Connecticut — Jessica G. Hynes

Federal — Mary Garvey Algero, Spencer L. Simons, Suzanne E. Rowe,
Scott Childs & Sarah E. Ricks

Florida, Third Edition, Revised Printing — Barbara J. Busharis
& Suzanne E. Rowe

Georgia — Nancy P. Johnson, Elizabeth G. Adelman & Nancy J. Adams

Idaho — Tenielle Fordyce-Ruff & Suzanne E. Rowe

Illinois, Second Edition — Mark E. Wojcik

Iowa — John D. Edwards, M. Sara Lowe, Karen L. Wallace
& Melissa H. Weresh

Kansas — Joseph A. Custer & Christopher L. Steadham

Kentucky — William A. Hilyerd, Kurt X. Metzmeier & David J. Ensign

Louisiana, Second Edition — Mary Garvey Algero

Massachusetts — E. Joan Blum

Michigan, Second Edition — Pamela Lysaght & Cristina D. Lockwood

Minnesota — Suzanne Thorpe

Missouri, Second Edition — Wanda M. Temm & Julie M. Cheslik

New York, Second Edition — Elizabeth G. Adelman, Theodora Belniak
& Suzanne E. Rowe

North Carolina — Scott Childs

Ohio — Katherine L. Hall & Sara Sampson

Oregon, Second Edition, Revised Printing — Suzanne E. Rowe

Pennsylvania — Barbara J. Busharis & Bonny L. Tavares

Tennessee — Sibyl Marshall & Carol McCrehan Parker

Texas, Revised Printing — Spencer L. Simons

Washington, Second Edition — Julie Heintz-Cho, Tom Cobb
& Mary A. Hotchkiss

Wisconsin — Patricia Cervenka & Leslie Behroozi

Wyoming — Debora Person & Tawnya Plumb

Louisiana Legal Research

Second Edition

Mary Garvey Algero

Suzanne E. Rowe, Series Editor

CAROLINA ACADEMIC PRESS

Durham, North Carolina

Library of Congress Cataloging-in-Publication Data

Algero, Mary Garvey.
    Louisiana legal research / Mary Garvey Algero. -- Second edi-
tion.
        pages cm
    Includes bibliographical references and index.
    ISBN 978-1-61163-248-4 (alk. paper)
    1. Legal research--Louisiana. I. Title.

    KFL75.A42 2013
    340.072'0763--dc23

                                        2013014819

                    CAROLINA ACADEMIC PRESS
                            700 Kent Street
                    Durham, North Carolina 27701
                    Telephone (919) 489-7486
                        Fax (919) 493-5668
                        www.cap-press.com

            Printed in the United States of America.

Dedication

*This book is dedicated to Chris, Elizabeth, Maggie, and Christopher Algero
and Joan and Walter Garvey.*

Summary of Contents

Contents

List of Tables, Figures, and Lagniappe

Tables

Figures

Lagniappe

Series Note

The Legal Research Series published by Carolina Academic Press includes titles from states around the country as well as a separate text on federal legal research. The goal of each book is to provide law students, practitioners, paralegals, college students, laypeople, and librarians with the essential elements of legal research in each jurisdiction. Unlike more bibliographic texts, the Legal Research Series books seek to explain concisely both the sources of state law research and the process for conducting legal research effectively.

Preface

This book is written to assist attorneys, law students, paralegals, librarians, and others in researching legal materials effectively and efficiently. While focused on Louisiana law, the book also provides the reader with information necessary to research federal law as well as the law of other jurisdictions.

In addition to discussing research techniques, sources, and strategies, the book highlights the unique characteristics of the Louisiana legal system, including the State's reliance on the Civil Code and statutory law and the value of precedent. The book also provides specific information on both print and electronic sources for locating law and provides legal citation information.

Discussion of research using electronic sources is meant to introduce basic features that researchers will encounter, not to exhaustively discuss all features of all electronic sources. As with most technologically based products, platforms for electronic research are always developing and changing. Fortunately, the vendors of online, commercial services provide training and tutorials to keep researchers up to date on their products. One of the decisions made in writing this book was to discuss basics regarding databases/sources selection on Westlaw and LexisNexis, even though these selections need not be made on WestlawNext and Lexis Advance. Decisions about what sources are best to use for research of particular issues must be made by the researcher at some point in the research process; thus, source selection is discussed for print and electronic research, even though the selection of types of sources to consider on WestlawNext and Lexis Advance may be made after a search is run.

Most citations in the book conform to the citation format for practitioners set out in the nineteenth edition of *The Bluebook: A Uniform*

System of Citation. Any variations from *The Bluebook*, such as to conform to Louisiana custom or rule, are noted within the text. Additionally, Appendix A compares the citation formats set out in *The Bluebook*, the *ALWD Citation Manual: A Professional System of Citation*, and Louisiana rules and customs.

Louisiana has a rich legal history, with its private law rooted primarily in French and Spanish traditions, many of which stem from ancient Roman law. In 1803, the United States purchased the territory of Louisiana, which included the land that is now the State of Louisiana. In that one year, this territory was governed successively by Spain, France, and the United States. The legal system that exists today has grown and has been most influenced by the traditions of these three nations.

Throughout this book, the reader will find text boxes that include historical notes of interest and quotes about Louisiana law and the Louisiana legal system. These additions are referred to herein as *Louisiana Lagniappe* (lanyap). *Lagniappe* derives from the Spanish *la ñapa*, which means *the gift*. Lagniappe was given its French spelling in southern Louisiana where the word is frequently used and refers to *something extra* or *a bonus* or *unexpected gift*. Enjoy this lagniappe while you learn!

Acknowledgments

Professor Suzanne E. Rowe, the Series Editor, significantly contributed to the quality of this book by reviewing and editing each chapter. Moreover, as the author of previous books in this series, Professor Rowe shared freely from her own body of work. In particular, the author acknowledges that Chapters 2, 10, and 11, and portions of Appendix A were based on Professor Rowe's book, *Oregon Legal Research*.

Additionally, the author acknowledges the contributions of the many Loyola law students who have informed her teaching of legal research and analysis over the years. In particular, she acknowledges the contributions of Nadia Hall, Bradley Driscoll, Raechelle Munna, Elisabeth Lorio Baer, Jason Baer, and Jennifer Englander, who assisted with the research for this book.

Further, the author acknowledges the generous support for research and writing provided by the administration, faculty, and staff of Loyola University New Orleans College of Law.

Louisiana Legal Research

Chapter 1

Fundamental Principles of Legal Research

I. Introduction

The fundamentals of legal research are the same in every American jurisdiction, though the details vary. While some variations are minor, others require specialized knowledge of the resources available and the analytical framework in which those resources are used. This book focuses on the resources and analysis required to be thorough and effective in researching Louisiana law. It supplements this focus with explanations of federal research and research into the law of other states, both to introduce other resources and to highlight some of the variations.

II. Intersection of Legal Research and Legal Analysis

The basic process of legal research is simple. For most print sources, you will begin with an index, find entries that appear relevant, read those sections of the text, and then find out whether more recent information is available. For most online research, you will search particular websites or databases using words likely to appear in the text of the relevant documents.

Legal analysis is interwoven throughout this process, raising challenging questions. In print research, where should you begin? Which words will you look up in the index? How will you decide whether an index entry looks promising? With online research, how will you choose relevant words and construct a search most likely to produce the documents you need? When you read the text of a document, how will you determine whether it is relevant to your client's situation? How will you learn whether more recent material changed the law or merely applied it in a new situation? The answer to each of these questions requires legal analysis. This intersection of research and analysis can make legal research very difficult, especially for the novice. While this book's focus is legal research, it also includes the fundamental aspects of legal analysis required to conduct research competently.

This book is not designed to be a blueprint of every resource in the law library or search engine on the Internet; many resources contain their own detailed explanations in a preface or a *Help* section. This book is more like a manual or field guide, introducing the resources needed at each step of the research process and explaining how to use them.

III. Intersection of Legal Research and Legal Tradition

The legal tradition in a particular jurisdiction — especially in Louisiana — is important to legal research. In discussing the role of tradition, the focus primarily turns to the types of legal authority in that jurisdiction, the structure of the judicial system, and the value or weight of those legal authorities when evaluating a case or legal issue based on that law. As a researcher, you will conduct legal research to determine what the law is on a topic or issue and how it should or will be applied by the courts of a jurisdiction. Sometimes your task will be simply to predict how the law will be applied, and sometimes your task will be to argue that the law should be applied in a particular way to reach a particular outcome. To accurately perform these tasks in your given jurisdiction, you need to understand these aspects of the legal tradition for the jurisdiction in which you are working and how these aspects may affect your research.

The legal traditions you will encounter as a researcher are the *common law tradition*, the *civil law* or *civilian tradition*, and a mix of the two.

Jurisdictions based on the common law tradition include England and other countries colonized by the English, including the United States and Australia. Jurisdictions based on the civil law tradition include most European countries, many Latin American countries, China, Japan, and many of the countries that arose from the former Soviet Union.

Louisiana is a *mixed jurisdiction*, blending characteristics from both the civilian tradition and the common law tradition. Other jurisdictions with mixed traditions include Canada, Scotland, South Africa, and Puerto Rico. In the early 1800s, after the United States purchased the territory that would become Louisiana, the people of this territory insisted on maintaining their civilian laws, which were mostly of Spanish and French origin. They rejected a complete adoption of the common law and common law methods that were used throughout the rest of the United States. However, the United States federal government set up a system of government and a judicial system in Louisiana to mirror the federal system and the systems in the other existing states. As a result, Louisiana private law, such as property law, family law, and tort law, remains based in the civilian tradition. Louisiana public law, such as criminal law, resembles and functions like the laws in the common law states and the federal government. More importantly, legal authorities are valued a bit differently in Louisiana than in the other forty-nine United States and in the federal legal system, as is discussed in Section V of this chapter.

A familiarity with the differences among legal traditions is essential to properly research and analyze the law, and this text will point out those differences between Louisiana and the other United States jurisdictions when appropriate.

IV. Basic Structure of Legal Systems in the United States

Louisiana is one of fifty states in the United States. The United States has a federal, or national, government, which includes a federal legal system. Each of the states has its own government, which includes its own legal system.

The United States, as well as each of the fifty states, has a constitution that provides for the basic structure of government and ensures certain rights to the people. A constitution takes precedence over all other sources of law, and the United States Constitution takes precedence over state constitutions.

The United States Constitution provides for a federal government that is divided into three branches—the legislative, the judicial, and the executive. All fifty states have a similar tripartite structure of government. These branches of government are the only institutions with the power and authority to make law in the United States. Constitutions[1] and statutes come from the legislative branch; cases are decided by the courts in the judicial branch; and administrative regulations, administrative agency decisions, and executive orders and proclamations come from the executive branch.

V. Types of Legal Authority

Legal authority refers to the law, as well as commentaries or discussions of the law. As a researcher, you need to know the value or weight of various legal authorities so that you will know how to use them and how a court in your jurisdiction will value and use the authorities.

If a legal authority comes from a lawmaking body acting in its lawmaking capacity, such as the legislature, it is considered *primary authority*; primary authority is *the law*. Primary authorities include constitutions, statutes, administrative regulations, executive orders and proclamations, municipal charters and ordinances, and judicial decisions. Everything else, that is legal authorities that come from a source other than a lawmaking body acting in its lawmaking capacity, is considered *secondary authority*. Secondary authorities include

---

1. Because constitutions in the United States set up the systems of government for particular jurisdictions, each of the original constitutions did not come from the legislature. However, amendments to constitutions ordinarily originate with the legislature of the jurisdiction, so they are listed here as being associated with the legislative branch of government. See Chapter 3, Part II.

publications such as law review articles, legal encyclopedias, restatements of the law, treatises, and practice materials. The authors of these documents are not writing with the power to make law; they are writing to explain the law, comment on the law, or advocate for what they think the law should be. Secondary authorities can be helpful to the researcher because they explain primary authorities and provide citations to primary authorities.

Primary and secondary authorities are also classified as mandatory or persuasive. *Mandatory authority* is a primary authority that is binding on the court before whom a dispute will be heard. If an authority is mandatory or binding, the court must follow and apply that authority to the dispute before it. In contrast, *persuasive authority* is a primary or secondary authority that does not bind the court before whom a dispute will be heard. Persuasive authority may include primary authority from jurisdictions other than where a dispute is pending and all secondary authority. In the absence of primary authority, courts will often look to persuasive authority for guidance.

A. Louisiana Legal Authority

Primary authority in Louisiana is dictated by the Louisiana Civil Code, which identifies the sources of Louisiana law as legislation and custom.[2] *Legislation* refers to "rules enacted by a person or group of persons enjoying legislative authority."[3] Legislation in Louisiana includes the United States Constitution, the Louisiana Constitution, Louisiana statutes, Louisiana Administrative Code provisions, executive orders and proclamations, and municipal charters and ordinances. The other source of law in Louisiana, *custom*, is said to result "from practice repeated for a long time and generally accepted as having acquired the force of law."[4] Although custom is identified as a source of law, few modern examples exist in which the courts have expressly

---

2. La. Civ. Code Ann. art. 1 (1999).
3. A.N. Yiannopoulos, *Louisiana Civil Law Systems Course Outline* 85 (1971).
4. La. Civ. Code Ann. art. 3.

cited custom as a basis for their decisions. However, the Louisiana Supreme Court and some legal scholars have indicated that modern examples of custom may arise from judicial decisions when the courts have consistently recognized a rule that is not found in legislation.

Although judicial decisions are not identified as a primary source of law by the Louisiana Civil Code, most Louisiana courts consider Louisiana Supreme Court decisions to be mandatory authority, *i.e.*, binding on Louisiana appellate and trial courts. Thus, in practice, Louisiana Supreme Court decisions are usually treated as mandatory authority. See Louisiana Lagniappe 1-1 for specific case references. Louisiana Courts of Appeal decisions are persuasive authority, not mandatory authority, but they are particularly persuasive to the district courts whose decisions these appellate courts will review.

Louisiana Lagniappe 1-1.

A Secondary Source Given Mandatory Authority?

The Louisiana Supreme Court has referred to its own prior decisions as "secondary information," and it has criticized an appellate court for treating prior decisions as primary authority. *Ardoin v. Hartford Accident & Indem. Co.*, 360 So. 2d 1331, 1334 (La. 1978). On the other hand, the court has explained that Louisiana appellate courts are bound to follow the Supreme Court's decisions. *Pelican State Assocs., Inc. v. Winder*, 219 So. 2d 500, 503 (La. 1969).

When Louisiana courts look to prior decisions on a particular legal issue, they are looking for examples of how Louisiana law, usually legislatively enacted law, has been interpreted and applied in the past to similar cases, as opposed to looking for a statement of a new law created by the court. The doctrine expressly recognized by Louisiana courts on the value of prior judicial decisions is the doctrine of *jurisprudence constante* or settled jurisprudence. This doctrine calls on courts to give great weight or persuasive value to an interpretation of a rule of law that has been accepted and applied by the courts in repeated decisions in a long line of cases.

The other force at work in determining the value of judicial decisions in Louisiana is the hierarchy of the court system. Like the majority of the court systems in the United States, including the federal court system, Louisiana has three primary levels of courts. District courts are the courts in which disputes are first filed and tried. If a party is unhappy with the result from the district court, the party may appeal that decision to the intermediate level of appeal, which is the Louisiana Court of Appeal. If a party wishes to appeal the decision of the court of appeal, the party may seek a review by the Louisiana Supreme Court.

This hierarchy of appeal and review means that the courts will always strongly consider the prior decisions of the courts to which their decisions will be appealed when rendering their decisions because they do not want the higher court to reverse their decisions. This practice has been referred to as *systemic respect for jurisprudence*,[5] and it seems to be present in most court systems where lower courts' decisions are reviewed by higher courts. Thus, regardless of whether prior court decisions are considered mandatory authority or persuasive authority, which remains an unsettled question in Louisiana, practically speaking they warrant the researcher's close attention and consideration when researching Louisiana law.

> **Louisiana Lagniappe 1-2.**
>
> **The Role of Judicial Precedent**
>
> "In the common law, judicial precedent plays a leading role, serving both as a source of law and as an example of a prior judge's methodology in reasoning from the case-law materials. On the other hand, a civil-law judicial precedent plays only a supporting role. The Civil Code is the primary source of law, and precedent serves merely as an example of a prior judge's interpretation and application of legislated law." James L. Dennis, *Interpretation and Application of the Civil Code and the Evaluation of Judicial Precedent*, 54 La. L. Rev. 1, 3 (1993).

Returning to the Civil Code's mandates on the sources of Louisiana law, in the absence of legislation and custom, the Civil Code instructs courts to consider *equity*, and it defines equity as "justice, reason, and prevailing usages."[6] When resorting to equity, the Louisiana judge should first look for other Louisiana legislation that

---

5. Mary Garvey Algero, *The Sources of Law and the Value of Precedent: A Comparative and Empirical Study of a Civil Law State in a Common Law Nation*, 65 La. L. Rev. 775, 781, 812–14 (2005).

6. La. Civ. Code Ann. art. 4.

could be applied by analogy to the issue before the court. When analogous provisions cannot be found, Louisiana judges have looked to prior decisions from Louisiana courts and other jurisdictions' courts, Louisiana doctrine, French doctrine, Roman law sources, and the judge's sense of justice. See Louisiana Lagniappe 1-2 above.

B. Legal Authority in Other American Courts

Primary authority in the other jurisdictions within the United States includes constitutions, statutes, administrative regulations, executive orders and proclamations, municipal charters and ordinances, and judicial opinions. The United States Constitution is the supreme law of the United States, and the state constitution is the supreme law of each state. If a statute is on point, that statute comes next in the hierarchy, followed by administrative rules, executive orders and proclamations, and municipal charters and ordinances. Judicial opinions may interpret these documents, but they cannot disregard them. A judicial opinion may, however, decide that a statute violates the constitution or that a rule oversteps its bounds. If there is no constitutional provision, statute, or administrative rule on point, the issue will be controlled by *common law*, also called judge-made law or case law.

The doctrine recognized by these courts on the value of prior judicial decisions, or *precedent*, is the doctrine of *stare decisis et quieta non movere*, which translates as "to stand by things decided and not disturb settled law."[7] In its broadest sense, it commands judges to apply the law as it has been set out in one prior case when the prior decision was made by a court that is higher than, and sometimes equal to, the court rendering the present decision.[8] In the federal court system, district courts are bound to follow the decisions of the United States Supreme Court and the United States Court of Appeals

---

7. Bryan A. Garner, *A Dictionary of Modern Legal Usage* 827 (2d ed. 1995).
8. *See* Alvin B. Rubin, *Hazards of a Civilian Venturer In Federal Court: Travel and Travail on the Erie Railroad*, 48 La. L. Rev. 1369, 1371 (1988).

to which its decisions are appealable. United States Courts of Appeals are bound to follow United States Supreme Court decisions. In the federal system, courts are not bound by the decisions of the courts at the same level, except that panels of United States Courts of Appeals are bound to follow the *en banc* decisions of their own court. In addition to stare decisis, the hierarchical nature of the court system causes lower courts to follow the decisions of higher courts that have the jurisdiction or power to review their decisions.

Stare decisis in the United States is not applied as rigorously as its definition implies. The United States Supreme Court has the power to overrule its own decisions, as do most state supreme courts. Moreover, federal courts and courts in the United States typically venture from strict adherence to precedent when the precedent is considered to be outdated, when "the existing rule has produced undesirable results," or when "the prior decision was based on what is now recognized as poor reasoning."[9]

---

9. Helene S. Shapo, Marilyn R. Walter & Elizabeth Fajans, *Writing and Analysis in the Law* 17 (5th ed. 2008).

Chapter 2

Overview of the Legal Research Process and Citation

I. Moving from Story to Strategy

The purpose of legal research is to solve a client's problem. Each client comes to a lawyer with a story; in telling the story, the client focuses on facts that are important to him, without regard to whether they are legally significant. The lawyer may need to ask questions to probe for facts the client may not immediately remember but which may have important legal consequences. The lawyer may also need to review documents such as contracts, letters, bills, or public records. It may also be necessary to interview other people who are involved in the client's situation.

In sifting through the client's story, the lawyer determines which legal issues are involved. Sometimes a lawyer cannot immediately identify the legal issues involved in a particular situation. Especially in an unfamiliar area of law, the lawyer may need to do some initial research to learn about the legal issues that affect the client's situation.

After understanding the facts and identifying the legal issues, the lawyer conducts research to determine what the law is and how to solve the client's problem.

This chapter introduces three concepts that are expanded in the remainder of the book. It introduces a six-step research process that can be adapted for most legal research projects. It explores when to research in print and online. It then concludes with an overview of legal citation.

II. Overview of the Research Process

Conducting effective legal research means following a process. This process leads to the authority that controls a legal issue as well as to commentary that may help you analyze new and complex legal matters. Table 2-1 provides an overview of the research process.

Table 2-1. Overview of the Research Process

1. Perform *pre-research tasks.* Gather facts, determine what your goals and objectives are in researching, decide which jurisdiction's law controls, generate a list of search terms, and develop a research plan.

2. Consult *secondary authorities* such as practice guides, treatises, legal encyclopedias, and law review articles. Secondary authorities explain the law and refer to primary authorities.

3. Find controlling *constitutional provisions, statutes,* or *rules* by reviewing their indexes or searching online for your search terms. Read these primary authorities carefully, update them if necessary, and then study their annotations for cross references to additional authorities and explanatory materials.

4. Find citations to cases by searching *digests* or *online databases.* A digest is essentially a multi-volume topic index of cases in a certain jurisdiction or subject area. Secondary authorities and research references in constitutions, statutes, and rules often contain citations to cases, as well. Read the cases either in *reporters* or online. A reporter series publishes the full text of cases in a certain jurisdiction or subject area.

5. *Update* legal authorities by using a citator such as *Shepard's Citations* or *KeyCite* to (a) ensure that an authority is still respected and (b) find additional sources that may be relevant to the research project.

6. *End your research* when you have no holes in your analysis and when you begin seeing the same authorities repeatedly.

This basic process should be customized for each research project. Consider whether you need to follow all six steps, and if so, in what order. If you are unfamiliar with an area of law, you should follow each step of the process in the order indicated.

Beginning your research with secondary sources will provide both context for the issues you must research and citations to relevant primary authority. As you gain experience in researching legal questions, you may choose to modify the process by moving directly to searching for primary sources. For example, if you know that a situation is covered by a statute, you may begin with that step. If you are given a citation to a relevant case, you might begin research with that case. Reading the case will send you to other relevant law through sources it cites. Updating the case will lead to other sources that cite to it. (For an historical view on the importance of updating, see Louisiana Lagniappe 2-1.)

A. Pre-Research Tasks

Before walking into the library or logging on to your computer, prepare for your research project by performing certain pre-research tasks. First, gather the facts of the client's situation. In law practice, gathering facts may include interviewing the client, reviewing documents, and talking to colleagues who are also working for the client. Be sure to get as accurate a picture of the facts as possible before you begin researching.

Second, determine the goals and objectives of your research. Decide or discern how long you have to work on the research project and what you plan to or are expected to produce as a result of your research. Is the research meant to comprehensively identify all of the law on an issue or is your research meant to be tailored to a discrete issue? Will you simply present your research to another person orally or will

---

Louisiana Lagniappe 2-1.

The Changing Law

"The growth of the law never stops. The mistake that all legislators make is to imagine that, by their codification, they establish it once and for all.... Nevertheless, the law changes every year, almost every day."

1 Marcel Planiol, *Treatise on the Civil Law* 69 (La. State Law Inst. trans., 12th ed. 1959).

you be expected to draft a memo summarizing the law and applying it to the client's facts?

The third part of pre-research is determining what jurisdiction's law controls your client's situation so that you know what law to research. Sometimes determining the governing law will be as easy as asking someone who is already working for the client, and sometimes determining the governing law may be an issue requiring its own research. You must determine whether federal law, the law of Louisiana or another state, or local law is applicable before you begin research.

The fourth part of pre-research is generating search terms. Search terms are the keys to unlocking almost any source in which you choose to research. Print sources will often have an index and a table of contents in which you will use your search terms to find relevant information. Researching electronically will require you to input search terms that are likely to appear in relevant documents, either in a synopsis of the document or the full text of the document. To generate a comprehensive list of terms, brainstorm your client's situation and write down all of the terms you can come up with before beginning to research.

Some researchers ask the journalistic questions: Who? What? How? Why? When? Where? Others use a mnemonic device like TARPP, which stands for Things, Actions, Remedies, People, and Places.[1] Whether you use one of these suggestions or develop your own method, generate a broad range of search terms regarding the facts, issues, and desired solutions of your client's situation. Include in the list both specific and general terms. Try to think of synonyms for each term because at this point you are uncertain which terms an index may include. Using a legal dictionary or thesaurus may help to generate additional terms.

B. Example of Generating Search Terms

Assume you are working for a defense attorney who was recently assigned to a burglary case. Around midnight, your client allegedly

---

1. *See* Steven M. Barkan, Roy M. Mersky & Donald J. Dunn, *Fundamentals of Legal Research* 15 (9th ed. 2009) (explaining "TARP," a similar mnemonic device).

used a crowbar to break the lock to an apartment, where he stole $4,000 worth of computer equipment. He is charged with aggravated burglary. You have been asked to determine whether there is a good argument for limiting the charge to simple burglary because he did not bring the crowbar with him into the apartment. Table 2-2 provides examples of search terms you might use to begin work on this project.

Table 2-2. Generating Search Terms

	Journalistic Approach
Who:	Thief, robber, burglar, property owner
What:	Burglary, aggravated burglary, simple burglary, crime
How:	Breaking and entering, crowbar, trespassing
Why:	Theft, stealing, stolen goods
When:	Midnight
Where:	Apartment, dwelling, home, household, inhabited dwelling
	TARPP Approach
Things:	Stolen goods, crowbar, computer equipment
Actions:	Burglary, breaking and entering, trespassing, damages, crime
Remedies:	Aggravated burglary, simple burglary, incarceration
People:	Thief, robber, burglar, property owner
Places:	Apartment, dwelling, home, household, inhabited dwelling

When brainstorming, the goal is to produce as many terms as possible. But when you begin researching, use those terms that appear on the list most often or that seem most important. As your research progresses, you will learn new search terms to include in the list and decide to eliminate others. For example, a secondary source may refer to a *term of art*, a word or phrase that has special meaning in a particular area of law. Later in your research, you may read cases that give you insights into the key words judges tend to use in discussing this topic. These terms and words need to be added to your list. You should also review the list periodically to help you refine your research. If an online search produces far too many results, review the list for more specific search terms. On the other hand, if the terms you use initially produce no hits, review the list for alternative, more general terms.

C. Develop a Research Plan

Effective and efficient legal researchers have a plan or strategy behind the steps they take to research the law. This final part of preresearch requires the researcher to consider the remaining five steps of the research process along with the following:

- what you already know about the issue and the area of law involved;
- what you already know about the types of sources that govern the issue;
- what resources you have readily available;
- which sources are best consulted in print and which sources are best researched electronically;
- how much time you have to complete the project;
- the purpose of the research, such as whether the research is to support legal analysis of a particular issue in a particular case or is to provide an in-depth explanation of an area of law; and
- how you will keep track and organize the materials you gather.

Considering these two lists together, you should write out a *research plan* before beginning research, identifying the steps you expect to take and the sources you expect to consult.

In addition to having a plan or strategy, effective and efficient researchers also approach their research tasks with a degree of flexibility that allows them to adapt their processes to the information they gather along the way. While researching, you may come across additional theories that support your client's case that need to be added to your research plan. Further, the sources in which you begin your research may refer you to other sources. Some examples follow:

Example 1: A secondary source refers you to what appears to be a controlling case on the issue. You should be flexible enough to move directly to that case, even though your plan directs you to research statutes first. If the case to which you are led is controlling, then it will reference any relevant statutes.

Example 2: You are given a citation to a controlling case to begin research. You should locate the case, then Shepardize or KeyCite the case for citations to additional authorities. You might also use the topics and key numbers in the case to locate additional citations in the appropriate digest. You may not need to consult secondary sources unless you still feel that you need more background or an overview of the issue.

Example 3: You are given or locate a citation to a relevant statute. You might use the annotations to the statute to locate cases interpreting the statute, or Shepardize or KeyCite the statute, to gather additional authorities that have cited the statute, including cases and law review articles.

Flexibility is also necessary to adjust to circumstances beyond the researcher's control. When lawyers or students use law school libraries or court libraries, sometimes the source to be consulted according to the research plan is not on the shelf. Some flexibility in a research plan will allow the researcher to adjust by either moving to the next source on the list or moving to electronic sources if appropriate. Having a written plan will also ensure that when the researcher departs from the plan, the researcher is able to refer back to the plan to make sure that all of the sources needed have been consulted to complete research.

D. Researching the Law

The remainder of this book explains how to use your search terms to conduct legal research in a variety of sources. Although the research process often begins with secondary sources, the book begins with primary authority because that authority is the goal of legal research. Chapters 3 and 4 address researching law that is enacted or adopted by a legislature, as well as researching court rules. These chapters include constitutional research, statutory research, research of ethics rules and court rules, and legislative history research. Chapters 5 and 6 address judicial systems and researching judicial decisions. Chapter 7 addresses researching administrative law and other executive documents.

After this focus on primary authority, Chapter 8 explains updating research using *KeyCite* and *Shepard's*. Chapter 9 explains how to research and use secondary sources and practice aids. Although each chapter includes information regarding online research for the specific source being discussed, Chapter 10 provides additional information for conducting legal research online. Chapter 11 should be consulted by the student or the researcher throughout the research process because it discusses strategies for researching and strategies for presenting legal arguments. Finally, Appendices A and B provide information on citation and selected websites of interest to the researcher, respectively.

III. Choosing to Research in Print or Online

Developing a comprehensive research strategy includes deciding when and how to best use print and online sources. Many researchers have a strong preference for online or print research. The best researchers, however, recognize that different formats are better for different types of resources and purposes. Often, the best researchers will move easily between online and print sources after considering answers to some of the questions set forth below. Ask yourself the following questions in deciding which sources to use at each step of your research. Often the best research strategy will include research using a combination of print and online sources.

A. Where Is the Document Available?

Recent primary authority is increasingly available both in print and online. Some important secondary sources may be available only in print, while some resources used to find and update the law are available only online. Do not assume that there is universal overlap between print and online sources.

B. How Fast and How Efficient Will Research Be?

Many researchers find that *beginning* legal research in print is more productive than beginning online because books tend to provide more context, which keeps the project focused. In addition, most attorneys find it easier to read more carefully and thoroughly in print than on a computer screen. Online research has a number of advantages, though, including the ease of searching and the convenience of downloading or printing important documents.

C. What Is the Document?

Novice legal researchers sometimes find it difficult to distinguish between different types of documents online. In print sources, different types of authorities often appear in separate books, making it easy to tell them apart. In contrast, many documents look the same on a computer screen. Moreover, hyperlinks in online sources allow you to jump from a case to a statute to an article in a few clicks. In an actual library, those moves may take you to different shelves or even different floors. If you favor the tactility of print research, you may prefer researching in a law library instead of online sources.

Additionally, government bodies often designate certain sources as "official" versions of the documents they produce, such as statutes, cases, and regulations. For research purposes and citation purposes, you should ensure that what you are looking at is from an official or reputable source.

D. Who Wrote the Document?

Be sure that you know who wrote a document before you base your analysis on it. Remember that only some documents are binding and authoritative. Documents written by legislatures, administrative agencies, and sometimes courts are "the law." Articles and treatises written by recognized experts in a field are not binding, but they can be very persuasive and are often authoritative. These types of documents are often available both in print and online. However, there are many other documents online with little or no authoritative value, and whose authors have only an ill-informed opinion to share. Know who the author is, and whether she has the reputation to give weight to her assertions.

E. How Accurate Is the Document?

Print material tends to be more accurate than online versions of the same documents. The very process of publishing, with its numerous stages of editing and revising, ensures a high level of reliability. In contrast, online material is often valued for the speed with which it becomes available. With this speed comes an inevitable sacrifice of accuracy; even reputable services post documents with less editing than a book would warrant. If you need to quote an authority, or are otherwise relying on very precise language from it, print sources are always preferable.

F. When Was the Document Published?

Print sources take longer to reach the researcher than online sources. To find the most current material, online sources often provide a clear advantage. But even websites may contain outdated material; you still need to determine whether an online document has a date indicating when it was posted or last updated. If no such date is available, at least note when you visited the website for reference later on.

When using an online database, you must also ensure that it covers a period of time relevant to your research. Online sources tend to cover more recent periods; thus, finding older material may require using print sources. A notable exception is HeinOnline, which makes available older law review articles that often are not included in other online sources.

G. How Much Context Is Provided?

Most print sources include tables of contents or outlines that provide an overview of the legal area. These tools can provide context so that a novice researcher can understand the big picture before concentrating on a narrow legal issue. An increasing number of online sources also provide these tools, and when searching online you should use them whenever they are available. Clicking on a table of contents link can show where a document is placed within related material. This tactic is especially helpful when an online search lands you in the middle of a single document and you lack the visual clues or the context to understand how that document relates to the bigger picture.

Many lawyers—from novices to experts—have stories about the great case or article that they stumbled across while looking for something else. These stories result not just from serendipity, but from using resources that put related information together. In the library, scan the books shelved nearby helpful sources, and skim through relevant books to see whether other sections are on point. Sometimes online searching also produces serendipitous results; if you feel you may be close to the exact material you need but cannot find it, try using an online table of contents link to reorient yourself.

H. How Much Does It Cost, and Who Is Paying?

Some sources are free to use. Print sources are "free" in the sense that the library has already paid for them. Online sources provided by governments and universities are also free. When cost is an issue, consider using these sources first.

Online research using commercial services, on the other hand, can be very expensive. A single research project, poorly conceived and sloppily done, can cost hundreds or even thousands of dollars. But never assume online research is *too* expensive—its efficiency is often worth its price. Moreover, many law offices are finding that they can negotiate reasonable flat rates that allow them access to the narrow set of online sources they use routinely in their practice.

Check the billing practices in your office before using commercial online sources: What is your office's contract with the online provider? How will your office pass along charges to clients? How much are the clients willing to pay? Will the office cover the costs of online pro bono work? Also, be sure you know your office's policy regarding the printing of online documents, which often brings extra charges.

IV. Legal Citation

Although you may not formally write up the results of your research immediately, when researching you need to be aware of what information you will need to gather about the sources you read to properly cite to those sources. If you record this information when researching, you will save yourself the trouble of having to retrace your steps to gather this information.

Proper citation to legal authorities is necessary to provide your reader with the information she needs to (1) find the authorities and (2) evaluate the value or weight of the authorities. Legal readers expect citations to be based primarily on the rules and the forms set out in *The Bluebook: A Uniform System of Citation*,[2] the *ALWD Citation Manual: A Professional System of Citation*,[3] or local citation rules governing the jurisdiction in which you are working. As a researcher you should determine which set of citation rules your reader prefers you to use, then use those rules. Although all of these sources are similar in the general information their citation forms convey, some differences exist among the forms for specific sources.[4]

For example, both *The Bluebook* and the *ALWD Citation Manual* generally follow the principle that single capitals in an abbreviation, except for abbreviations in periodical names, are not separated from

---

2. *The Bluebook: A Uniform System of Citation* (Columbia Law Review Ass'n et al. eds., 19th ed. 2010).

3. ALWD & Darby Dickerson, *ALWD Citation Manual: A Professional System of Citation* (4th ed. 2010).

4. Most citations in this book conform to the citation form for practitioners set out in *The Bluebook* unless indicated otherwise.

each other by a space, and a single capital combined with an ordinal contraction, like 2d or 3d, is treated as a single capital.[5] Thus, in accordance with this principle, the following abbreviations are properly spaced: S.W.2d, F.3d, and N.E. On the other hand, a capital letter joined with a lower case letter in an abbreviation is separated by a space from a single capital letter and from another capital with a lower case letter as follows: So. 2d, F. Supp. 2d, and S. Ct. Despite the consistency of this rule among the two primary citation manuals, many attorneys and judges in Louisiana omit the space between So. and 2d in practice, and the Louisiana Supreme Court omitted the space in its rule dictating a public domain citation form for documents submitted to Louisiana courts.[6] Thus, many judges and attorneys in Louisiana use So.2d to abbreviate the *Southern Reporter, Second Series.*

Another example of a variation in citation format is guided by the type of document in which the citation will be placed and the citation manual being used. *The Bluebook* includes a section referred to as *Bluepages*, which provides rules specific to the citation forms to be used in documents written for law practice, including rules governing the typeface to be used in these documents. The rest of the *The Bluebook* is directed at citation conventions for law review documents. The rules dictate different typeface conventions for these documents. The *ALWD Citation Manual* does not vary typeface conventions by the type of document. One of the main differences resulting from these variations is that under *The Bluebook* large and small capitals must be used for parts of citations for law review documents, *e.g.*, Law Review, while practitioner documents use regular font. In the *ALWD Citation Manual*, large and small capitals are never used.

Later chapters in this book will point out the specific citation rules for authorities as they are discussed. However, this section identifies some of the general citation rules for various sources according to *The Bluebook* and the *ALWD Citation Manual*, as well as some specific Louisiana rules and practices. This section is written to make the re-

---

5. *Bluebook* Rule 6.1; *ALWD* Rule 2.

6. *See* La. Sup. Ct. Gen. admin. Rules pt. G, r. 8. An example of the format dictated by this rule is found below in Part IV.C on cases.

searcher aware of the type of information necessary to be collected for proper citation of each source. It is not meant to replace using one of these citation manuals to precisely identify proper abbreviations, spacing rules, and proper typeface conventions to be used in the various citation forms. Be aware that not all of the examples below are accurate for all three citation manuals; some minor variations exist and can be explored by referring to the rules included in footnotes.

A. Constitutions

When citing to constitutions, a citation will include an abbreviated name of the constitution and the article, amendment, or section being cited. If the cite is to a current version of the constitution, no date is given. A date is provided if the cite is to an out of date version of the provision.[7]

Examples: La. Const. art. 5, § 5(A).

U.S. Const. amend. I.

B. Legislation

Cites to statutes will include an abbreviated name of the code or book in which the statute is found; the title, article, section, or chapter being cited; and the date of the book or supplement to the book in which the current version of the statute is found. Additionally, some citations will require identification of the book's publisher.[8]

Examples: La. Civ. Code Ann. art. 3 (1999).

La. Rev. Stat. Ann. § 9:2794 (2009).

28 U.S.C. § 1331 (2006).

---

7. *Bluebook* Rule 11 and T1; *ALWD* Rule 13 and Appendix 1.

8. *Bluebook* Rule 12, Bluepages B6, and Table T1; *ALWD* Rule 14 and Appendix 1.

C. Cases

Case citations will include the name of the case, with certain words abbreviated based on the citation manual's abbreviation rules; the volume of the reporter in which the case is found; the abbreviated name of the reporter; the page number of the first page of the case; the page number on which particular information is found; the name of the court properly abbreviated; and the year of the decision.[9] Some citation rules, like part G, rule 8, of the Louisiana Supreme Court General Administrative Rules, also require the docket number of the case and the month and date of the decision for case citations in documents submitted to the court.[10]

Examples: *Boudreaux v. Thibodaux*, 341 So. 2d 99, 104
(La. 1972).
Frank v. Times Picayune, Inc., 119 F.3d 12,
19–21 (5th Cir. 2003).
Pennoyer v. Neff, 95 U.S. 714 (1877).
Smith v. Jones, 93-2345 (La. 7/15/94); 650
So.2d 500.[11]
Smith v. Jones, 93-2345 (La. App. 1 Cir.
7/15/94); 650 So.2d 400.

D. Administrative Regulations

When citing to administrative regulations, include the title number, the abbreviated name of the publication in which the regulation is found, the part or section being cited, and the date of the book or

---

9. *Bluebook* Rule 10, Bluepages B5, and Tables T1, T6, and T10; *ALWD* Rule 12 and Appendices 1, 3, and 4.

10. La. Sup. Ct. Gen. Admin. Rules pt. G, r. 8. This rule applies to the citation of Louisiana cases decided after December 31, 1993.

11. This case citation and the following citation follow part G, rule 8 of the Louisiana Supreme Court General Administrative Rules, which requires a docket number and no space between So. and 2d.

supplement to the book in which the current version of the regulation is found.[12]

Examples: La. Admin. Code tit. 11, § 9 (2004).

11 C.F.R. § 391 (2005).

E. Books and Periodicals

A book citation may include the book's author; title; volume number, if the book is one in a multi-volume series; a pinpoint reference to the pages, sections, or paragraphs on which the researcher found particular information; editor; translator; edition; publisher; and copyright date.[13]

ALWD Example: Kathryn Venturatos Lorio, *Louisiana Civil Law Treatise: Successions & Donations* vol. 10, § 2.2 (2d ed., West 2009).

Bluebook Example: 10   Kathryn   Venturatos   Lorio, *Louisiana Civil Law Treatise: Successions & Donations* § 2.2 (2d ed. 2009).

When citing to an article in a periodical, a citation may include the author, the title of the article, the volume number of the periodical, the abbreviation of the periodical, the page on which the article begins, a pinpoint reference to the page on which the researcher found the particular information for which he is using the article, and the date.[14]

Example: Monica Hof Wallace, *Child Support Savings Accounts: An Innovative Approach to Child Support Enforcement*, 85 N.C. L. Rev. 1155, 1165 (2007).

---

12. *Bluebook* Rule 14 and Table T1; *ALWD* Rule 19 and Appendix 1.

13. *Bluebook* Rule 15 and Bluepages B8; *ALWD* Rule 22.

14. *Bluebook* Rule 16, Bluepages B9, and Table T13; *ALWD* Rule 23 and Appendix 5.

Chapter 3

Researching Enacted Law: Constitutions, Statutes, and Rules

I. Introduction

This chapter focuses on researching law that has been enacted or authorized by a legislative body. Discussion includes constitutional research, statutory research, and research of ethics rules and court rules.

The United States Constitution is the "supreme Law of the Land," and it takes precedence over all other sources of law in the United States. It sets up the structure of the federal government, and the various state constitutions set up the structure of those states' governments. The federal government and each state in the United States have enacted a code or set of statutes, which are primary sources of law. Additionally, courts in each jurisdiction, with authority granted to them by constitutions or statutes, have drafted court rules to govern practice and procedure in the courts.

In Louisiana, Article 1 of the Louisiana Civil Code identifies legislation, or enacted law, as the primary source of law in Louisiana. The various titles of the sources of Louisiana enacted law are listed in Table 3-1, along with the terms used for designating provisions in citations. The Louisiana Constitution takes precedent over all other laws in the state, much like the provisions of law in Louisiana must be consistent with and not contradict the provisions of the United States Constitution. Additionally, the Louisiana Constitution grants to the Louisiana Supreme Court the power to make rules to govern the courts. Exercising this power, the Louisiana Supreme Court created the Rules of the Louisiana Supreme Court,

Table 3-1. **Titles of the Sources of Louisiana Enacted Law**

Louisiana Constitution of 1974 (articles)
Louisiana Constitution Ancillaries (articles and sections)
Louisiana Civil Code (articles)
Louisiana Revised Statutes (titles and sections)
Louisiana Code of Civil Procedure (articles)
Louisiana Code of Criminal Procedure (articles)
Louisiana Code of Evidence (articles)
Louisiana Children's Code (articles)

the Uniform Rules of the Louisiana Courts of Appeal, and the Louisiana Rules for District Courts.

All Louisiana enacted law is published in a series of books identified as *West's Louisiana Statutes Annotated* (LSA), which are sometimes familiarly referred to in Louisiana as "the green books" because of their green covers. The LSA is the official publication of Louisiana laws.[1] This series of books is updated through the use of *pocket parts* and *supplements*, which are published annually, as well as softbound supplements to the pocket parts, which are published throughout the year.

A pocket part is an update to a bound book, published in pamphlet form and placed in a pocket inside of the back cover of the book. A supplement is a softbound update to a hardbound volume that, like a pocket part, provides updated material to the hardbound volume. A supplement is used instead of a pocket part when the amount of material to be included in the update is too great to include in a pocket part, and the publisher is not yet ready to publish an updated hardbound volume. A careful and efficient researcher will always check the pocket part or supplement of a book to determine whether any provisions in the book have been amended, repealed, or otherwise modified.

Another feature of the LSA is that it is *annotated* as opposed to *unannotated*. An unannotated version of enacted laws includes the

---

1. In 2004, *LexisNexis Louisiana Annotated Statutes* was published for the first time. Like the LSA, this publication includes an annotated version of all Louisiana enacted law.

laws only, without commentary or references to other sources. An unannotated version of enacted laws can be helpful to the researcher who would just like to see the laws, in succession, without the visual interruption of additional material.

On the other hand, an annotated version of the laws is especially helpful to the researcher who is exploring the meaning of the laws. The LSA provides the following *annotations* after each enacted law to the extent such material is available: historical notes tracing the development of the law, cross references to related enacted laws, law review references, library references to the West Key Number Digests, Westlaw topic numbers, legal encyclopedia references, and *Notes of Decisions*. Notes of Decisions are references and citations to cases in which the enacted law has been mentioned, discussed, or interpreted.

This chapter will discuss each compilation of enacted law and rules and explain how to effectively research these materials.

II. Constitutional Research

A constitution in the United States is a document that recognizes and preserves individual rights and liberties, provides a structure for government, and determines how members of the government will be selected. As he prepared to serve as a delegate to the convention that drafted the Louisiana Constitution of 1921, Louisiana judge and Loyola law professor Richard A. Dowling described the purpose of a constitution when he wrote, "[T]he function of Constitution builders is not to enact laws, but to embody, co-ordinate and define the principles by which laws shall be made and administered. Constitutions are not statutes. A written Constitution consists of fundamental organic articles determining the legislative, the judicial and the executive organism."[2]

All other laws in the United States must be consistent with and not violate the United States Constitution, and all other laws in each individual state must be consistent with and not violate their own state constitutions. If a law or judicial decision violates the principles set

---

2. Richard A. Dowling, Editorial, 2 Loy. L.J. 36, 39 (1921).

Table 3-2. Articles of the Louisiana Constitution of 1974

Article 1.	Declaration of rights
Article 2.	Distribution of powers
Article 3.	Legislative branch
Article 4.	Executive branch
Article 5.	Judicial branch
Article 6.	Local government
Article 7.	Revenue and finance
Article 8.	Education
Article 9.	Natural resources
Article 10.	Public officials and employees
Article 11.	Elections
Article 12.	General provisions
Article 13.	Constitutional revision
Article 14.	Transitional provisions

out in the United States Constitution or in a governing state constitution, a court may pronounce that law or decision *unconstitutional*, which would make the law or decision unenforceable.

A. Louisiana Constitution

1. Background

In accordance with the ideals of what a constitution should include, the current Louisiana Constitution addresses these fundamental principles and more. It declares the fundamental rights of the people, it establishes the structure of the state and local governments in Louisiana, and it prescribes the methods by which members of the government will be selected. It also creates the power to tax and raise revenue, provides for a public education system, addresses issues of the ownership and protection of natural resources, and prescribes the method for amendment of the Constitution itself. The articles of the Louisiana Constitution of 1974 are listed in Table 3-2.

The first Louisiana Constitution, which borrowed heavily from the constitution in force in Kentucky at the time, was adopted in 1812. The constitution currently in force, Louisiana's tenth constitution, is the Constitution of 1974, which is the result of a constitutional convention that convened in 1973 to frame a new state constitution. See Louisiana Lagniappe 3-1. One hundred and five delegates were elected to the constitutional convention, one from each of the Louisiana districts. An additional twenty-seven delegates were appointed by the governor.

> **Louisiana Lagniappe 3-1.**
>
> **Louisiana Constitutions**
>
> The Louisiana Constitution of 1974 replaced the Louisiana Constitution of 1921 and its 536 amendments. The Constitution of 1921 and its amendments became known as the longest state constitution ever written.

The constitution was approved by the people of Louisiana in a special election, and it became effective on December 31, 1974. Amendments to the constitution require ratification by a two-thirds majority vote of the Louisiana House of Representatives and the Senate as well as a majority vote from Louisiana voters and a proclamation by the governor.

A document related to the Louisiana Constitution of 1974, but whose provisions do not have the weight of constitutional provisions, is the Louisiana Constitution Ancillaries. The ancillaries are provisions of the Louisiana Constitution of 1921 that were not included in the Constitution of 1974, but that were continued as statutes. These statutes were not subsequently incorporated into the Louisiana Revised Statutes, nor were they repealed. These statutes may be researched in the same way as the Constitution.

2. Researching the Louisiana Constitution

The Louisiana Constitution is published in a number of places, in print and online. However, you should begin research in a source that has a comprehensive index. In Louisiana, this source is the LSA, which provides an annotated version of the Louisiana Constitution of 1974 and the Louisiana Constitution Ancillaries and two indices that include references to the constitution and the ancillaries.

First, to research only the Louisiana Constitution or its ancillaries, the most efficient index to use is the index that follows the constitution and the ancillaries. This index provides citations to the

Louisiana Constitution and the Louisiana Constitution Ancillaries only. Second, to find any and all Louisiana enacted provisions on a particular issue, use the general index to the LSA, which provides citations to all Louisiana enacted sources, including the constitution and its ancillaries. These indices are updated using pocket parts or supplements, which should be checked to locate additional index entries.

After locating the correct index, use the search terms you have generated to locate citations to relevant provisions; then pull the provisions referenced to determine if the provisions are applicable to the research question. In addition to reading the text of the constitutional provision or provisions located to determine relevancy, also consider the descriptions of cases accompanying case citations in which the constitutional provision has been interpreted or discussed. These references help to give some context and meaning to broadly stated provisions. You may also find citations to secondary sources that may explain the provision as well as citations to related provisions.

The LSA also allows a researcher to compare versions of the Louisiana Constitution. If you are interested in comparing the Louisiana Constitution of 1921 with the Constitution of 1974, tables that precede the current constitution include this information. A Disposition Table indicates what happened to 1921 constitutional provisions when the 1974 Constitution was enacted, including whether the provision was included in the 1974 Constitution and where it was included or whether the provision was eliminated. A Derivation Table provides the reverse of this information, showing the researcher from which provisions of the 1921 Constitution current provisions were derived.

Locating the Louisiana Constitution online is simple. A number of free online sources provide the text of the constitution, and these sources can be accessed using a search engine like Google or Yahoo! and the search terms *Louisiana Constitution*. The Louisiana State Legislature's free web portal, located at www.legis.state.la.us, allows a researcher to view a list of the various titles of the articles of the constitution as well as search for particular words found in the constitution or its ancillaries. If you know the citation to a provision, enter the citation to see the full text of that provision.

The constitution and the ancillaries can also be located and researched online for a fee using the Westlaw or LexisNexis services. Provisions of the constitution and its ancillaries may be located on these services by entering their citations. Additionally, you may search the databases that include Louisiana statutes, which also include the constitution and its ancillaries, using search terms in a terms and connectors or a natural language search. You may also search the table of contents of these documents, and on Westlaw you may search the index of the LSA.

To locate and focus only on constitutional amendments, go to a comprehensive list on the Louisiana State Legislature's web portal, located at www.legis.state.la.us. From "Louisiana Laws," this site allows the researcher to view a list of all proposed constitutional amendments to the Louisiana Constitution of 1974, including information such as the date the amendment was proposed, by whom, and whether it passed or failed. A print source in which to find amendments that were adopted in a given year is the *Acts of the Legislature*. An adopted amendment to the constitution is first published in the volume of the *Acts of the Legislature* for the session following the date of the election during which the amendment was approved by the voters. Otherwise, amendments to the constitution will be reflected in the updated version of the constitution.

3. Updating Louisiana Constitution Research

When researching in the LSA, be sure to check any pocket part or supplement to the printed version of the constitution to ensure that you are looking at the most up-to-date version of the provision. Additionally, Shepardize or KeyCite the provision, using LexisNexis or Westlaw, to determine if any changes have occurred since the printed version was published. When locating provisions using a free online source, be sure to update as previously mentioned to ensure that the provision located is up to date.

B. The United States Constitution and Other State Constitutions

Like the Louisiana Constitution, the United States Constitution and other state constitutions are available both in print and online. Researching these constitutions will require that the researcher follow steps similar to the steps outlined for researching the Louisiana Constitution. Most state constitutions are available in annotated print versions with indices, which is the best place to begin research for those unfamiliar with the provisions that may govern their research questions.

The United States Constitution is available in the *United States Code Annotated* and the *United States Code Service*, which both provide annotated versions of the United States Constitution. It is critical that a researcher of United States constitutional law read annotations, case interpretations, and commentary in secondary sources to understand the meaning of constitutional provisions. These publications also include annotated versions of all federal statutes, which are discussed in more detail later in this chapter. These publications have a separate index for the United States Constitution immediately following its text, as well as a general index, which allows the researcher to search for all federal statutes and federal constitutional provisions in the same index. The LSA includes the United States Constitution and a separate index for the Constitution, as do most states' annotated codes.

The Constitution is also widely available online, through both free and fee-paid services. Some online services only allow you to view the Constitution, while others, including the fee-paid services, allow you to search for provisions by citation and by search terms and allow you to search and view annotations to the constitutional provisions.

III. Statutory Research

Almost any area of law in Louisiana will be governed by a statute in some way. A statute may govern the rights of the parties or their duties toward each other, define what behavior is criminal and what the penalties are for that behavior, or even prescribe the time period in which a person has to bring an action against another person. In every United States jurisdiction, statutes are primary authority. They are mandatory authority and binding on a court if (1) the statute was effective at the time relevant to the issue and (2) the statute is part of the law that governs the case in which the issue has arisen. Thus, a researcher is wise to research statutes at the start of a project not only to determine what statutes might potentially govern the issue, but also to gather citations to other sources that interpret the statutes, such as cases and secondary sources.[3]

Statutes are published in three forms. They are first published as *slip laws*, which are individual statutes identified by their law or act numbers just after passage by the legislature. They are next published as *session laws*, in a compilation of all laws passed in a particular legislative session. Session laws are usually organized chronologically. Third, statutes are published in a code, which includes all statutes governing in a particular state or in the federal system. Codes are organized by subject or topic, with new statutes from a legislative session integrated into an already existing code. Researching slip laws and session laws will be discussed in Chapter 4. Researching statutes that have been published as part of a code is discussed below.

A. Louisiana Statutory Research

1. Background

In Louisiana, where the primary sources of law are legislation and custom, the importance of identifying legislation or enacted law is paramount. The Louisiana legislative branch is charged with enacting Louisiana statutory law. Like its federal counterpart, the Louisiana legislature is comprised of the state House of Representatives and the

---

3. Of course, the researcher may find that a research question is governed exclusively by common law or that the courts have developed an extensive doctrine beyond statutory law. Thorough research will include case research, which is discussed in Chapters 5 and 6, as well as statutory research.

Louisiana Lagniappe 3-2.

Louisiana Statutory Law

Commenting on the role of statutory law in Louisiana, then-Chief Justice of the Louisiana Supreme Court, the Honorable John A. Dixon, Jr., wrote: "The attitude toward statutory materials is ... one of the outstanding differences between the common law and civil law systems.... Our Civil Code defines law as the solemn expression of the *legislative* will.... Legislative supremacy in Louisiana is more than theoretical; it is factual." John A. Dixon, Jr., *Judicial Method in Interpretation of Law in Louisiana*, 42 La. L. Rev. 1661, 1662 (1982) (citing La. Civ. Code art. 1 (1870)).

---

state Senate. These bodies enact law that is published as part of one of the following six titles: (1) the Louisiana Civil Code; (2) the Louisiana Revised Statutes; (3) the Louisiana Children's Code; (4) the Louisiana Code of Evidence; (5) the Louisiana Code of Civil Procedure; and (6) the Louisiana Code of Criminal Procedure. All law enacted by the legislature must be approved by the governor. The terms *enacted law, statutory law,* or *statute* are often used generically to refer to law that is enacted by a legislature, even though these terms may refer to compilations known as codes or revised statutes, as is the case in Louisiana. See Louisiana Lagniappe 3-2.

A powerful group involved in the drafting and passage of Louisiana law that works closely with the Louisiana legislature is the Louisiana State Law Institute (Law Institute), a group charged with law reform in Louisiana. Although not a part of the legislature, the Law Institute was created by the legislature "to promote and encourage the clarification and simplification of the law of Louisiana and its better adaptation to present social needs; to secure the better administration of justice and to carry on scholarly legal research and scientific legal work."[4]

The Law Institute is influential in the process of lawmaking in Louisiana, especially through its proposals of new legislation and legislative revision, its members' testimony before legislative committees, and its commentary that follows statutory provisions. The Law Institute maintains committees to study and propose amendments in

---

4. La. Rev. Stat. Ann. §24:204(A) (2007). For other provisions regarding the Law Institute, see also La. Rev. Stat. Ann. §§24:201–:208, :251–:256.

various fields of law. Further, Law Institute committees study newly enacted legislation to ensure that provisions throughout Louisiana enacted law are consistent and work together. The Law Institute produces a Biennial Report to the legislature on its work, which can be found on its website, www.lsli.org.

a. Louisiana Civil Code

The Louisiana Civil Code is a set of laws or rules that governs a person's interactions with other people. Colonel John Tucker introduced the Civil Code as follows:

> "It is your most important book because it ushers you into society as a member of your parents' family and regulates your life until you reach maturity. It then prescribes the rules for the establishment of your own family by marriage and having children, and for the disposition of your estate when you die, either by law or by testament subject to law.
>
> It tells you how you can acquire, own, use, and dispose of property onerously or gratuitously.
>
> It provides the rules for most of the special contracts necessary for the conduct of nearly all of your relations with your fellowman ... ; and, finally, all of the rights and obligations governing your relations with your neighbor and fellowman generally."[5]

The predecessor to the Louisiana Civil Code, the *Digest of the Civil Law Now in Force in the Territory of Orleans (Digest)*, was enacted in 1808. The *Digest* was enacted after the people of the Territory of Orleans, the portion of the newly acquired Louisiana territory that later became the State of Louisiana, successfully convinced authorities to allow them to retain their civil laws and not adopt the common law used in the rest of the United States. The *Digest* borrowed heavily from the French Code Napoleon, as well as from Spanish, Roman,

---

5. A.N. Yiannopoulos, *An Introduction to The Louisiana Civil Code*, in La. Civ. Code Ann., at XV (1999) (quoting John H. Tucker, Jr., *Foreword*, in La. Civ. Code Ann., at XXI (1993)).

and English law. Following the *Digest* came the Louisiana Civil Codes of 1825, 1870, and the Civil Code currently in place, which has been revised in parts since the 1960s. In honor of the Bicentennial of the Louisiana Civil Code, copies of the *Digest* in French, the language in which it was originally written, and in English translation, with notes made by the drafters, have been made available online at www.law.lsu.edu/index.cfm?geaux=digestof1808.default. This online version is also searchable.[6]

A review of the table of contents of the current Civil Code reveals its breadth and confirms Professor Tucker's description of the Code as a document that governs all facets of our private lives. It is divided into a preliminary title and four books, including: Book I, Of Persons; Book II, Things and the Different Modifications of Ownership; Book III, Of the Different Modes of Acquiring the Ownership of Things; and Book IV, Conflict of Laws. A code like the Louisiana Civil Code "is not intended to provide for every contingency that might arise. It is a statement of general principles that are to be applied by deduction or analogy to particular cases.... In the civil law the function of the court is one of interpretation."[7]

b. Louisiana Revised Statutes

The Louisiana Revised Statutes currently include fifty-three titles that are organized by topic.[8] These topics are arranged alphabetically, as shown in Table 3-3. The Louisiana Revised Statutes tend to be worded more specifically than are the Civil Code provisions. Further, in addition to Title 9, several of these provisions supplement portions of the Civil Code. Title 9 of the Louisiana Revised Statutes, which is also known as the *Civil Code Ancillaries*, supplements the Civil Code

---

6. For an interesting discussion of the history of the Civil Code, see A.N. Yiannopoulos, *Requiem for a Civil Code: A Commemorative Essay*, 78 Tul. L. Rev. 379 (2003).

7. John H. Tucker, Jr., *The Code and the Common Law in Louisiana*, 29 Tul. L. Rev. 739, 757–58 (1955).

8. Titles 5, 7, and 55 were repealed and have not been replaced, which is the reason those numbers are missing from the list in Table 3-3.

Table 3-3. Titles of the Louisiana Revised Statutes

Title 1.	General Provisions	Title 31.	Mineral Code
Title 2.	Aeronautics	Title 32.	Motor Vehicles and
Title 3.	Agriculture and Forestry		Traffic Regulation
Title 4.	Amusements and Sports	Title 33.	Municipalities and
Title 6.	Banks and Banking		Parishes
Title 8.	Cemeteries	Title 34.	Navigation and Shipping
Title 9.	Civil Code Ancillaries	Title 35.	Notaries Public and
Title 10.	Commercial Laws		Commissioners
Title 11.	Consolidated Public	Title 36.	Organization of the
	Retirement Systems		Executive Branch of
Title 12.	Corporations and		State Government
	Associations	Title 37.	Professions and
Title 13.	Courts and Judicial		Occupations
	Procedure	Title 38.	Public Contracts, Works
Title 14.	Criminal Law		and Improvements
Title 15.	Criminal Procedure	Title 39.	Public Finance
Title 16.	District Attorneys	Title 40.	Public Health and Safety
Title 17.	Education	Title 41.	Public Lands
Title 18.	Louisiana Election Code	Title 42.	Public Officers and
Title 19.	Expropriation		Employees
Title 20.	Homesteads and	Title 43.	Public Printing and
	Exemptions		Advertisements
Title 21.	Hotels and Lodging	Title 44.	Public Records and
	Houses		Recorders
Title 22.	Insurance	Title 45.	Public Utilities and
Title 23.	Labor and Workers'		Carriers
	Compensation	Title 46.	Public Welfare and
Title 24.	Legislature and Laws		Assistance
Title 25.	Libraries, Museums,	Title 47.	Revenue and Taxation
	and Other Scientific and	Title 48.	Roads, Bridges and
	Cultural Facilities		Ferries
Title 26.	Liquors–Alcoholic	Title 49.	State Administration
	Beverages	Title 50.	Surveys and Surveyors
Title 27.	Louisiana Gaming	Title 51.	Trade and Commerce
	Control Law	Title 52.	United States
Title 28.	Mental Health	Title 53.	War Emergency
Title 29.	Military, Naval, and	Title 54.	Warehouses
	Veterans' Affairs	Title 56.	Wildlife and Fisheries
Title 30.	Minerals, Oil, and Gas		
	and Environmental		
	Quality		

and follows the same overall structure as the Civil Code in its division into four books.

c. Other Louisiana Enacted Law

The other statutory compilations, including the Louisiana Children's Code, the Louisiana Code of Evidence, the Louisiana Code of Civil Procedure, and the Louisiana Code of Criminal Procedure, include law on topics that are self evident from their titles. These codes provide law on these specific topics that should be read in conjunction with relevant provisions of the other codes, which is why consulting a comprehensive index is usually the best way to proceed with research.

Notably, the Louisiana Code of Evidence, the Louisiana Code of Civil Procedure, and the Louisiana Code of Criminal Procedure are styled as *codes* as opposed to *rules*, and these codes have all been enacted by the Louisiana legislature. As explained in Section IV.A of this chapter, the federal counterparts to these codes are styled as rules and they are created by a Supreme Court-appointed committee, pursuant to power given to the Court by Congress.

2. Researching Louisiana Statutes

a. Researching in Print Sources

The best place to begin research to locate relevant statutes published in any of the Louisiana statutory compilations is the LSA, which is the official publication of Louisiana enacted law. If the researcher is given a citation to a statute, she will locate the volume of the series that contains that particular statutory compilation and that provision, then locate the provision. The spine of each volume identifies which statutory compilation is included in that volume and which titles, chapters, articles, or sections are contained in the volume.

Thus, if you are given a citation to a Civil Code article, such as La. Civ. Code Ann. art. 2315, you must make sure that the volume of the LSA you pull contains the Civil Code as opposed to the Code of Civil Procedure. You must also make sure that the volume contains the article identified because the Civil Code spans more than one volume. If you are given a citation to a section in the Louisiana Revised Statutes, you will have a citation that includes the title number of the revised statute as well as the section, which will look like the following: La. Rev. Stat. Ann. §25:1 or R.S. 25:1. You will locate the volume of the LSA that includes that particular title and section of the Revised Statutes.

Once the correct provision is located, you will want to check both the hardbound volume containing the provision as well as any pocket part or supplemental softbound volume to ensure that you are looking at the correct version of the article as well as the most up-to-date annotations to the article. If the statute printed in the main volume has been amended in any way, the publisher may reprint the entire amended statute in the pocket part or supplement or it may just reprint the sections that have been amended, leaving the unamended portion in the main volume. (Tip: Checking the pocket part *first* will allow you to find out immediately if the statute in the hardbound volume has been amended or replaced by a more recent version so that you do not waste time considering an obsolete version.) Even if the statute has not been amended, the publisher will include updates to the annotations in the pocket part, such as recent cases.

If you are not given a citation to a statute, but are given the facts of a case and an issue, you should locate the two volumes of the General Index to the LSA, and use the search terms you have generated to locate citations to relevant provisions. See Chapter 2 for some ideas on generating search terms. You should record the citations identified through use of your search terms, as well as use any alternative terms suggested in the index to locate citations to additional provisions.

Then, you should locate these provisions to determine if they are applicable to the research question. In addition to carefully reading the text of the identified provision or provisions located to determine relevancy, you should also consider the Notes of Decisions. The Notes of Decisions include a short description of a point of law in a case, followed by the name of the case, an abbreviated reference to the court that decided the case and when the case was decided, and an abbreviated citation to the case. These references can help to give some context and meaning to broadly stated provisions. The annotation may also include citations to secondary sources that may explain the provision as well as citations to related provisions.

For example, a researcher trying to locate a statute governing tort liability in Louisiana will probably find a reference to Louisiana Civil Code Article 2315 using search terms in the General Index. When this statute is located in print, the researcher will find that immediately preceding the statute is a designation that indicates that this article is part of Chapter 3, which is entitled *Of Offenses and Quasi Offenses.*

A table of contents accompanies the title, which indicates that Articles 2315 through 2324 relate to liability and damages. Article 2315 does not include the word "tort," but it reads in part, "Every act whatever of man that causes damage to another obliges him by whose fault it happened to repair it." The article is followed by 668 pages of annotations, including historical and statutory notes, cross references, references to law review and journal commentaries, library references, and Notes of Decisions in which the statute has been applied and interpreted.

The Notes of Decisions are so voluminous that they have their own table of contents or index. Typically, the first few Notes of Decisions address the statute's validity and its general application and construction. Turning to the first few Notes of Decisions, the researcher finds a reference to a case in which the note indicates that "this article presents the foundation upon which all tort law in Louisiana has been constructed." BINGO! The researcher now knows that this statute is what she is looking for, and she is ready to dig in to the Notes of Decisions and its table of contents to locate discussions of the statute that show its application to facts similar to her case. She has also benefitted from the table of contents to the chapter, which provides her with related provisions.

Most statutes or code provisions will not be accompanied by annotations of such great length. But the lessons from above are that (1) the researcher should carefully read the provision located; (2) the researcher should consider the material surrounding the statute, such as chapter or section headings and related provisions; and (3) the researcher should consult the annotations, especially the Notes of Decisions, to determine how the statute has been interpreted or applied in past cases.

Once a relevant statute has been located, the researcher should continue by locating and reading cases in which the statute has already been interpreted and applied. The Notes of Decisions are not law and should never be cited. They are meant to give the researcher sufficient information to decide whether and how to locate the noted decisions.

In some circumstances, a statute may be commonly known by a name or descriptive term, such as the *Child Custody Jurisdiction and Enforcement Act* or *Lemon Law*. The LSA has a Popular Name Table that follows the General Index listings. If a statute is known by a popular name, the name will appear along with the citation to the statute.

b. Researching Online

You may also research Louisiana statutory compilations online. The Louisiana State Legislature's free web portal, www.legis.state.la.us, allows you to view a list of the various statutory compilations and choose to either see a provision by typing in its citation, view the table of contents of a particular compilation, or search one or more statutory compilations using search terms. The provisions on the legislature's website are not annotated.

Louisiana statutes can also be located and researched online for a fee using the Westlaw or LexisNexis services. Statutes may be located by citation or you may use search terms to search the databases on these services that include Louisiana statutes using terms and connectors or natural language. Additionally, you may view the table of contents of all or of select statutory compilations by selecting the Louisiana statutory database, selecting the statutory compilations in which you are interested, and choosing *TOC*. Westlaw also allows you to search the index to the statutes, which is the same as the print version of the LSA General Index referenced above, and to search the Popular Name Table.

For the novice researcher or the researcher unfamiliar with a particular area of law, the best place to start researching is in the LSA index. When researching statutes, an online terms and connectors search of the text of the statutes is not always an effective method of research because its success depends on whether the researcher was lucky enough to choose the same words as the legislature for her search. It also often yields results beyond the target material, which then requires the researcher to spend extra time weeding through irrelevant statutes.

3. Updating Louisiana Statutory Research

When researching in the print version of the LSA, check any pocket part or supplement to the volume in which the statute is located to ensure that you are looking at the most up-to-date version of the statute. Additionally, always use LexisNexis or Westlaw to Shepardize or KeyCite statutes found using any methods to determine if any changes have occurred since the source consulted was printed or posted and to determine whether the statute has been declared unconstitutional. See Chapter 8 for more information on updating.

4. Interpreting and Applying Louisiana Enacted Law

As has been previously mentioned, when researching Louisiana law you should always locate any and all enacted law that governs the issue before you. You should first look to legislative sources for provisions that are directly applicable to your research question, then you should look for provisions that are relevant and applicable by analogy if no directly applicable provisions are found.

When it comes to interpreting and applying the law, the Louisiana legislature has enacted law on this subject as well.[9] "Leg-

---

9. La. Civ. Code Ann. arts. 9–13 (1999); La. Rev. Stat. Ann. §§ 1:3–:4 (2003).

islation is a solemn expression of legislative will."[10] Thus, to carry out that will, the interpretation of enacted law in Louisiana requires a consideration of the legislature's intent.[11] The court must begin the process of determining the legislative will or intent by looking to the plain language of the enacted law. "When a law is clear and unambiguous and its application does not lead to absurd consequences, the law shall be applied as written and no further interpretation may be made in search of the intent of the legislature."[12] The Louisiana Supreme Court has abided by this rule, even in circumstances when a plausible argument could be made that the legislature did not intend what appeared to be the statute or constitutional provision's plain meaning.[13]

Other principles that govern statutory interpretation include the following: (1) "words of a law must be given their generally prevailing meaning";[14] (2) words are to be given the meaning that "best conforms to the purpose of the law";[15] (3) words that are ambiguous are to be examined within the context of the law in which they are found;[16] (4) it is presumed that every word in a statute has a purpose;[17] and (5) "[l]aws on the same subject matter must be interpreted in reference to each other."[18] These principles of interpretation apply to articles of the Louisiana Constitution, as well as to statutes.[19]

Keeping these principles in mind, the researcher should ordinarily begin any written analysis of Louisiana law by quoting the enacted law that governs the issue. If only a part of a longer provision is rel-

---

10. La. Civ. Code Ann. art. 2 (1999).

11. *City of New Orleans v. La. Assessors' Ret. & Relief Fund*, 986 So. 2d 1, 16–17 (La. 2007).

12. La. Civ. Code Ann. art. 9; *see also* La. Rev. Stat. Ann. § 1:4.

13. *See, e.g., City of New Orleans*, 986 So. 2d at 22.

14. La. Civ. Code Ann. art. 11.

15. *Id.* art. 10.

16. *Id.* art. 12.

17. *City of New Orleans*, 986 So. 2d at 17.

18. La. Civ. Code Ann. art. 13.

19. *City of New Orleans*, 986 So. 2d at 15.

evant, the researcher might simply quote the relevant part of the provision and either omit the other portion or paraphrase it. Then, if the statute has already been interpreted by a court or courts, the researcher should move to a discussion of the interpretation. Custom, equity, and secondary sources may also factor into the analysis, as is discussed in Chapter 1.

B. Federal Statutory Research and Statutory Research in Other States

1. Background

The United States Congress is the legislative branch of government charged with the task of enacting statutes. Congress is made up of the House of Representatives and the Senate, which are two separate bodies. A bill produced in one of these bodies becomes law only after it is passed or voted on positively by a majority in each body of Congress and is approved by the president. If a bill is vetoed by the president, it may still become law if two-thirds of Congress votes for its passage despite the presidential veto. See more on this subject in Chapter 4 on legislative history research. All other state governments have a similar legislative branch of government.

2. Researching Federal Statutes

Researching federal statutes, as well as the statutes of other states, is similar to researching Louisiana statutes. You will generate search terms to use in a print or online index for the jurisdiction's code or you will use an online service to search the appropriate database using terms and connectors or natural language. You may consult a popular name table to locate a statute that is known by a particular name, and you may consult the table of contents of the statutes in print or online.

Federal statutes are codified in the United States Code, which is published in the publication by the same name, the *United States Code* (U.S.C.). The U.S.C. is the official publication of federal laws. A new set is published every six years and supplemented during the interim by cumulative annual supplements. The U.S.C. has an extensive index, but it is not annotated.

Federal statutes are also published in the *United States Code Annotated* (U.S.C.A.) and the *United States Code Service* (U.S.C.S.). The U.S.C.A. is available in print and online on Westlaw. The U.S.C.S. is available in print and online on LexisNexis. These publications are a good place to begin researching because they are annotated. Thus, they include historical notes on the statute, cross references to other relevant statutory provisions, Notes of Decisions providing information on cases in which the statute has been discussed or referenced, and references to secondary sources that discuss the statute. They are also supplemented more often than is the U.S.C.

After locating the General Index for the publication you have chosen, locate your search terms to find citations to relevant statutes. The references will include a reference to the title in which the statute is found as well as to the section number that identifies the statute. The United States Code is divided into fifty subject titles. You must be sure to locate the correct title and section of the statute identified in the index. If you are working in print documents, you will then check the main volume of the code as well as any pocket part or supplement to the volume of the code to obtain the statute.

For example, the statute granting the federal district courts subject matter jurisdiction over cases involving diverse parties is found in Title 28, Section 1332, of the United States Code. The subject of Title 28 is *Judiciary and Judicial Procedure*. Section 1332 is found in Chapter 85 of the title, but the chapter will not be referenced when citing the statute by title and section nor will it be referenced in the index as a means of finding the section. The statute will be cited to the most recent edition of the U.S.C. as 28 U.S.C. § 1332 (2006).

If you are given a public law number or a popular name of a federal statute to begin research, the sources mentioned above publish tables that allow you to look up the statute by its public law number or by its popular name or its short title to obtain a citation to the statute by title and section.

Once you locate the statute, preferably in the U.S.C.A. or the U.S.C.S., read the statute carefully and consider annotations to determine if the statute may govern your issue or legal question, in the same way that you did for Louisiana statutory research.

The United States Code is also available online on several websites. In addition to the fee-based services, Westlaw and LexisNexis, free online access is available. The Office of the Law Revision Counsel of the United States House of Representatives, which is charged with keeping an official codification of United States laws, maintains a free website on which it posts the United States Code. On this site, the Code is searchable by citation and by using terms and connectors. This unannotated version of the Code is consistent with the official printed version of the United States Code. The website may be accessed at http://uscode.house.gov/lawrevisioncounsel. shtml. Additionally, the Government Printing Office's online Federal Digital System (FDsys) provides the full text of the current United States Code and its annual supplements.

3. Researching Other States' Statutes

Research for statutory provisions in other states is similar to the method outlined above for locating Louisiana and federal statutes. A citation manual, such as the *ALWD Citation Manual* or *The Bluebook*, is a good resource to use to identify the name of the publication in a particular state in which that state's statutes are published. Each of these manuals has an appendix or table on United States jurisdictions that identifies publications for each state. Moreover, a search on an Internet search engine will also yield the names of state statutory publications as well as websites on which state statutes are published. When you have identified the correct state publication, turn to the state publication's general index or employ the other methods discussed above for conducting Louisiana legal research, but tailor them to the state in which you are researching.

4. Updating Federal and State Statutory Research

In addition to checking for pocket parts and supplements to the volumes in which statutes are located, you should Shepardize or

KeyCite statutes, using LexisNexis or Westlaw, to determine if any changes have occurred since the printed version was published and to determine if the constitutionality of the statute has been questioned.

IV. Researching Court Rules and Ethics Rules

A. Court Rules

The term *court rules* may be used to refer to two types of rules: (1) state or federal procedural or evidentiary rules, and (2) rules established by a particular court or courts that supplement state or federal procedural rules, sometimes known as *local rules*.

1. Procedural and Evidentiary Rules

The first type of rules includes state or federal rules of civil or criminal procedure, which dictate procedures that must be used to file documents and litigate in a particular jurisdiction's court system. These rules identify the types of pleadings that may be filed, the style of those pleadings, when and how parties must be served with process, what parties may be joined in actions, how discovery is to be conducted, various motions that may be filed, and procedures involving juries, just to name some of the topics covered. They also include state or federal rules that identify the types of evidence that can be admitted in court and how litigants go about introducing evidence in court, among other things.

In Louisiana, the Louisiana Code of Civil Procedure, the Louisiana Code of Criminal Procedure, and the Louisiana Code of Evidence are enacted by the legislature and are considered primary authority. They are published with other Louisiana enacted laws in the LSA and may be researched like other Louisiana enacted law, as is discussed above in Part II of this chapter.

The Federal Rules of Civil Procedure, the Federal Rules of Criminal Procedure, the Federal Rules of Appellate Procedure, the Federal Rules of Evidence, and the Federal Rules of Bankruptcy Procedure are also published with the federal statutes in the U.S.C., the U.S.C.A., and the U.S.C.S. The first four sets of rules are published with Title 28 of the United States Code in the U.S.C. and the U.S.C.A., and the bankruptcy rules are published with Title 11 of the United States Code in these publications. The U.S.C.S. publishes separate volumes devoted to rules that follow the titles of the United States Code. You may research these rules using the General Index to these publications of the United States Code or using the separate indices that follow each set of rules. These rules are also readily available online, both on free and fee-based web services.

These federal rules are promulgated in a unique way, unlike federal statutes. Through the Rules Enabling Act,[20] Congress has authorized the judiciary to prescribe rules of practice, procedure, and evidence to govern in the federal courts. Acting under this authority, the Supreme Court has created the Committee on Rules of Practice and Procedure, which in turn appoints subcommittees to review these rules, entertain comments on the rules and on rule changes, and recommend changes to the Supreme Court. If the Court approves proposed rules, they are sent on to Congress. They become effective if Congress does not act to reject or modify them within a certain period of time.

2. Court-Specific Rules or Local Rules

The second type of court rules are sometimes referred to as local rules. These procedural rules originate in particular courts and govern filings and appearances in those courts only. They supplement the procedural rules discussed above and often provide more detail about how to proceed in a particular court. The United States Supreme Court Rules, for example, dictate the number of copies of documents to be filed with the Court, how those documents should be styled, and the requirements for admission to appear before the Court, among other things. The Louisiana Supreme Court has a similar set of rules.

---

20. 28 U.S.C. §§ 2071–2077 (2006).

Appellate courts and district courts within a court system may have a set of rules that govern all courts at the same level within that system, often styled *uniform rules*, as well as local rules that are particular to each court. For example, the Uniform Rules of Louisiana Courts of Appeal govern in all Louisiana intermediate appellate courts, and each appellate circuit has its own set of local rules. The Rules for Louisiana District Courts are supplemented by local rules for each district.

Similarly, the Uniform Local Rules of the United States District Courts for the Eastern, Middle, and Western Districts of Louisiana include uniform rules as well as rules that are designated to apply only in certain districts. The United States Court of Appeals for the Fifth Circuit has its own set of rules to supplement the Federal Rules of Appellate Procedure mentioned above, and the United States Bankruptcy Courts for the Eastern, Middle, and Western Districts have each promulgated local rules to supplement the Federal Rules of Bankruptcy Procedure.

Local rules are frequently found on court websites, in West deskbooks (which are updated annually), and in annotated codes. Table 3-4 provides a list of Louisiana and federal courts and identifies where their rules are published.

B. Ethics Rules

The legal profession is a self-policing and self-regulating profession that is governed by state codes of professional conduct or ethics. The American Bar Association publishes the Model Rules of Professional Conduct, which the majority of states have adopted in some form. These rules only become applicable to lawyers in a state when they are adopted by the state legislature, the state supreme court, or the state bar association.

The Louisiana Rules of Professional Conduct are patterned on the Model Rules. They were adopted in 1986 by the Louisiana Supreme Court and reenacted in 2004. The Louisiana Constitution, Article 5, Section 5, gives the Louisiana Supreme Court jurisdiction over disci-

Table 3-4. Locating Local Rules

Court	Where Rules Are Published
Louisiana State Courts	• www.lasc.org/rules • *Louisiana Rules of Court, State* (West) • LSA volume designated as *Court Rules*, which follows La. Rev. Stat. Ann. title 13 • Westlaw and LexisNexis
United States Supreme Court	• www.supremecourt.gov/ctrules/ctrules.html • U.S.C., U.S.C.A., and U.S.C.S. • Westlaw and LexisNexis
United States Fifth Circuit Court of Appeals	• www.ca5.uscourts.gov/clerk/docs/5thCir-IOP.pdf • *Louisiana Rules of Court, Federal* (West) • Westlaw and LexisNexis
United States District Courts for the Eastern, Middle, and Western Districts of Louisiana	• www.laed.uscourts.gov/LocalRules/LocalRules.htm • www.lawd.uscourts.gov/local-rules/ • *Louisiana Rules of Court, Federal* (West) • Westlaw and LexisNexis
United States Bankruptcy Courts for the Eastern, Middle, and Western Districts of Louisiana	• www.laeb.uscourts.gov/RuleOrders/pdf/LocalRules/050113.pdf • www.lamb.uscourts.gov/localrules.htm • www.lawb.uscourts.gov/court/Publications/LocalRules/LocalRules02052010.pdf • *Louisiana Rules of Court, Federal* (West) • Westlaw and LexisNexis

plinary proceedings against members of the bar and gives the court the power to regulate members of the bar. The legislature expressly gave the Louisiana Supreme Court the power to create and regulate the Louisiana State Bar Association as a state corporation.

Pursuant to these grants of power, the court created the Louisiana State Bar Association, and the court prescribes the rules governing the profession. These rules have the force and effect of substantive law. The legislature has enacted some statutes governing the profession as well. Legislation is found in Louisiana Revised Statutes Title 37, which governs Professions and Occupations. Section 211 of Title 37 begins the statutes governing attorneys. An appendix following the statutes includes the Rules of Professional Conduct, which are part of the articles of incorporation of the Bar Association.

When researching ethical questions in Louisiana, the researcher may use her search terms in the Title 37 index or the LSA General Index to locate references to statutes and rules relevant to the legal question presented, either in print or online, similar to statutory research discussed earlier in this chapter. Additionally, the Rules of Professional Conduct have a good table of contents that can help the researcher pinpoint applicable rules.

Secondary sources that are particularly helpful on this topic include *Louisiana Lawyering*, which is part of the *Louisiana Civil Law Treatise* series, and *Louisiana Professional Responsibility Law and Practice* by Dane Ciolino. Additionally, the *Restatement of the Law Third: The Law Governing Lawyers*, addresses ethics issues and applications of rules across the Unites States. Researching in secondary sources is discussed in Chapter 9.

Further, because the Louisiana Rules of Professional Conduct are based on the Model Rules of Professional Conduct, consideration of the official comments to the Model Rules of Professional Conduct can also be helpful. The Model Rules and comments are available online on the American Bar Association's website at www.americanbar.org/groups/professional_responsibility/publications/model_rules_of_professional_conduct.html. The Louisiana Rules can be accessed at the Louisiana Disciplinary Board's website, which also has Louisiana Supreme Court opinions, Disciplinary Board Recommendations, and other documents relevant to the ethical practice of law in Louisiana. The Board's website is www.ladb.org. These rules are also available on Westlaw and LexisNexis.

Chapter 4

Bill Tracking and Researching Legislative History

This chapter addresses the legislative process, *bill tracking*, and *legislative history* research. Bill tracking refers to following the progress of a bill through the legislative process before that bill is published in a code. You may need to track a bill for a client who has an interest in potential changes in the law, perhaps because she is in the midst of contract negotiations that could be affected by changes. You may also need to track a bill to find out the contents of a newly enacted statute that has not yet been published in a code.

Legislative history research refers to the reverse of that process—that is, it refers to looking back at the process by which a bill became a law, usually to gather information about the legislative intent behind the law. You may need to do this close in time to the law's passage or many years after.

I. The Legislative Process in Louisiana

Understanding the legislative process is fundamental to researching legislation. The Louisiana legislature is one of three branches of government authorized by the Louisiana Constitution.[1] The legislature is charged with enacting laws and setting policy for the state. The legislature also oversees certain actions of the executive branch, such

---

1. *See* La. Const. Ann. art. III.

as reviewing administrative rules of executive branch agencies. It is composed of the Senate, which is authorized to have a senator from each senatorial district, not to exceed thirty-nine, and the House of Representatives, which is authorized to have a representative from each representative district, not to exceed one hundred and five. The legislature meets annually in regular session, and from time to time meets in an extraordinary session at the behest of the governor or a majority of each elected house.

The process by which a bill becomes a law in Louisiana is similar to the process employed by the federal government and by many other state legislative bodies. The idea for a bill may come from a citizen, a citizen's group, a legislator, a legislative committee, or the Louisiana State Law Institute, which is discussed in Chapter 3. Figure 4-1 shows the progress of a bill through both houses of the Louisiana legislature and on to the governor for signature or veto.

At each step of the process, information is generated that may be valuable in determining the status of a bill or legislative intent. For example, to determine legislative intent, compare the various versions of the same bill as it works its way through the process or read or listen to minutes of a committee hearing or floor debate. This information may be accessed through the Louisiana legislature's website, from the House or Senate docket, or from the Louisiana secretary of state's office, as is set forth below in more detail.

II. Bill Tracking in Louisiana

Lawyers advise clients about upcoming changes in the law that may affect a client's business; they serve as lobbyists who are involved in advocating for or against the passage of a new law; and they serve as legislators. These are just a few roles in which bill tracking may be necessary.

To track any bill introduced in Louisiana since 1997, begin by going to the homepage of the Louisiana legislature at www.legis.state.la.us. The acts from a legislative session are published online throughout the legislative session. Begin your search by either scrolling down to the section entitled *Bill Search* or clicking on *Session Info*, which is located on

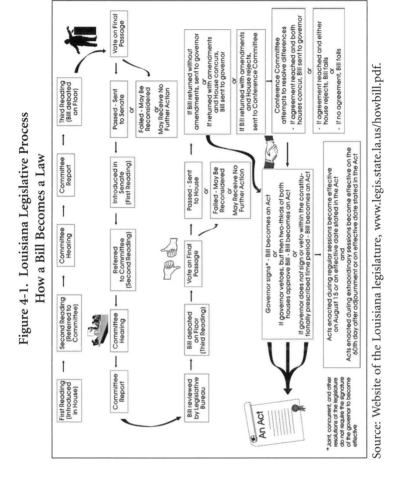

Figure 4-1. Louisiana Legislative Process
How a Bill Becomes a Law

Source: Website of the Louisiana legislature, www.legis.state.la.us/howbill.pdf.

the navigation bar at the top of the page. Select the legislative session in which you are interested. Then, search a bill in one of seven ways:

1. By a specific instrument's bill number;
2. By the author's name;
3. By a range of instruments (*e.g.*, House bills starting with HB22);
4. By date, if you know the specific date on which legislative action was taken;
5. By a committee to which a bill has been referred;

6. By a text search of the entire instrument database (this method is best if you do not know the specific bill number);
7. By manually searching the *Subject Index to Bills*, a document that is located under *Key Session Information*.

Once you have chosen a specific bill, there are several options from which to choose:

1. View the current version of the bill;
2. View a list of all versions of the bill;
3. View a list of all amendments to the bill;
4. View the digest, which provides a short explanation of the bill;
5. View the votes on all actions concerning the bill;
6. View the history of the bill, which provides all information from the introduction to the final action taken on the bill.

Louisiana Lagniappe 4-1.

Public Update Legislative Services Line

The Louisiana House and Senate operate a telephone line that can be used by the public to speak to legislative staff about bills, committee activity, and aspects of the legislative process. The Public Update Legislative Services Line (PULS line), can be reached at 342-2456 for calls originating in Baton Rouge, and (800) 256-3793 for calls originating outside of the Baton Rouge calling area.

The Louisiana legislature's website is easy to use, there is no fee associated with its use, and it is frequently updated. Both Westlaw and LexisNexis also have databases devoted to Louisiana bill tracking that allow searching and are updated frequently. Of course, these services are fee-based. Westlaw's coverage spans from 1997 forward, while LexisNexis's coverage spans from 1999 forward. See Louisiana Lagniappe 4-1 for information on a telephone service provided by the House and Senate.

Louisiana acts are also published in print in *State of Louisiana: Acts of the Legislature* and *West's Louisiana Session Law Service*.[2] The first

---

2. LexisNexis has recently begun publishing legislative acts in *Louisiana Advance Legislative Service*.

referenced publication may take a year or more to be printed, while the West publication may take up to three months from the date an act is approved to arrive in the library. These *session laws* are published by legislative session in the order in which they were enacted, and they are designated by act number and corresponding bill number. *West's Louisiana Session Law Service* also provides a table listing existing Louisiana laws that are affected by the session laws.

A citation to a session law is to the year of the session, the publication in which it appears, and the page number on which it appears. For example, Act number 739 of the 2006 legislative session would be cited as follows: 2006 La. Acts 2654-55, or 2006 La. Sess. L. Serv. 1830-31 (West). Note that in the second citation, *The Bluebook* dictates that you add a parenthetical following the page number indicating West as the publisher of the *Louisiana Session Law Service.*

III. Louisiana Legislative History Research

The *legislative history* is the record of all legislative actions that transpired in passing a law. You might need to compile a legislative history as you seek to determine the meaning of a statute.[3] To compile the legislative history of a Louisiana law, you must know the session of the legislature in which it was enacted and the original act number. This information can be obtained by locating the statute, article, or rule, which is discussed in Chapter 3. Following the statute, article, or rule, an indication of the year of the legislative session and an act number, such as Acts 1986, No. 697, will be provided.

If the provision you are researching was enacted in 1997 or later, the best place to research legislative history is on the Louisiana legislature's website referenced above.[4] If the provision is an older provision, use print sources.

---

3. But see Chapter 3, Part III, Section A.4 for a discussion of the limitations on the use of legislative intent to argue statutory meaning.
4. As with bill tracking, both LexisNexis and Westlaw have databases that provide legislative history on Louisiana law for a fee.

If researching on the legislature's website, follow these steps to locate legislative history:

1. Click on *Session Info* on the navigation menu at the top of the screen, then select the legislative session in which the law you are researching was passed.

2. Under the title *Bill Search for (year) Session* bar, click on the pull-down box accompanying the designation *View a specific instrument*, which has the letters *HB* as a default. Select the word *Act*. Type in the act number, then click on the box marked *View*.

3. The next screen will show the original House or Senate bill number, the author of the act, a brief summary of the act, and its status. Below this information are links, which provide important information. See Figure 4-2 for an example of this screen.

This information can be valuable for discerning the intent behind laws. The *Text—All Versions* link allows you to see and compare each version of the bill as it made its way through both chambers of the legislature. If the bill was suggested by the Louisiana State Law Institute, comments by the Law Institute accompany the bill. These comments are not part of the enacted law, but they may assist in determining legislative intent. The *Digest* link identifies for each version of the bill what the present law provided and what the proposed changes were meant to accomplish. The *History* link provides a dated record of all actions involving the act, from filing through signature by the governor. The *Amendments* link provides the text of every adopted committee amendment for the act as well as every proposed floor amendment.

A legislative history can also be done in print sources.

1. Locate the *Resumé* for the year in which the act was passed. The Resumé provides a list of all acts passed during a session with their original house or senate bill numbers.

2. Armed with the bill number, consult the *Legislative Calendar* for the year in which the act was passed. Locate the bill number in the Legislative Calendar and find a chronological history of the bill as it made its way through the legislative process. Additionally, find references to session *Journal* pages

Figure 4-2. Example of Screen with Links to History and Amendments

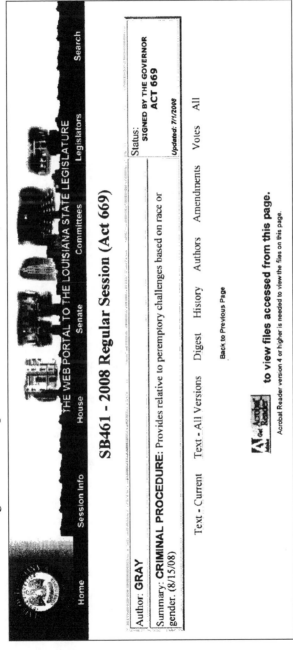

Source: Louisiana legislature website, www.legis.state.la.us, for Act 669 of the 2008 Regular Session.

where more details about action taken and amendments made are recorded. Each legislative body keeps its own Journal, arranged chronologically. See Louisiana Lagniappe 4-2, which provides an excerpt from the House Journal.

Louisiana Lagniappe 4-2.

House Journal Excerpt

An excerpt from a speech the governor made to the House at the start of the legislative session: "During the last session of Congress [a delegation from Louisiana] ... went to Washington ... to lay before our representatives and before Congress the condition of the levees, and the inability of the State to rebuild and maintain them, with a view of inducing the government to take upon itself the rebuilding and maintenance of the larger levees as a national work." La. H. J., Sess. of 1875, Reg. Sess. at 8 (Jan. 4, 1875) (speech by Governor William P. Kellogg). Note the date of the legislative session.

The best places to find these print sources for legislative history research are parish libraries, the four Louisiana law schools' libraries, and most Louisiana court libraries. Note that older materials may only be available in the Law Library of Louisiana, and some very old materials may only be available in French.

In addition to the above, minutes or audio recordings of legislative committee meetings regarding the law you are researching can be helpful. The *dockets* of the House and Senate provide minutes from committee meetings for a fee.[5] Video and audio recordings of House committee meetings and chamber proceedings from 1999 forward are available through the House website at http://house.louisiana.gov. Some are available directly through the website, and some must be requested. Video and audio recordings from the Senate are available from 2008 forward on the Senate's website at http://senate.legis.state.la.us/default.asp. Audio recordings of committee meetings that pre-date the above may be available by request from the research library of the Louisiana State Archives.

---

5. The term docket is used here to indicate the central repository kept by each chamber where official legislative instruments and publications are kept. Contact information is as follows: House Docket—(225) 342-6458; Senate Docket—(225) 342-2365.

Other sources for determining the intent of the law are *exposé des motifs* and minutes of Law Institute meetings. *Exposé des motifs* analyze recommended changes to the law and explain the reasons for the particular changes. They are produced by the Law Institute to accompany the revision of a title of the Civil Code or a chapter of the Revised Statutes. They can be found in the LSA publication of Louisiana laws prior to the title or chapter to which they correspond; they are not part of the law. Minutes of Law Institute meetings may be obtained from the Law Institute.

Finally, if you are researching a Civil Code provision, the *2008 Compiled Edition of the Civil Codes of Louisiana*, edited by A.N. Yiannopoulos, provides the official text of the Louisiana Civil Code of 1870, as revised and amended through the 2008 legislative session. It provides a rich source of legislative history on Civil Code articles. This three-volume set is part of the LSA. It also includes official texts of the Louisiana Civil Codes of 1808 and 1825.

IV. The Federal Legislative Process

The federal legislative process is similar to the state process, with the exception that documents associated with the federal legislative process are more readily available than are similar documents in most states. Federal statutes begin as bills, usually originating in one chamber of Congress. A bill from the House of Representatives will be designated with an *H.R.* preceding its number, while a Senate bill will be designated with an *S.* preceding its number. When a bill becomes a law, it receives a public law number, such as P.L. 101-336. The first number indicates the session of Congress in which the law was enacted, and the second number indicates the chronological number of the law from that session.

Subsequently, the law is published in the *United States Statutes at Large* with all laws from the session, and its citation is to the volume of this publication and the page number on which the law appears in the publication. Laws are published chronologically in this publication. The law referenced above is known as the *Americans with Dis-*

abilities Act (ADA), which was passed in 1990 during the 101st Congress. Its citation in the *Statutes at Large* is 104 Stat. 328.

The law enacted is eventually published in the *United States Code* in the title or titles and sections that correspond to its subject matter. The first section of the ADA is codified in Title 42, which is the title covering Public Health and Welfare. It can be found in 42 U.S.C. § 12101.

For more information on the federal legislative process, see documents written by the parliamentarians of the House of Representatives and the Senate, which can be found on the Library of Congress's website at http://thomas.loc.gov, under the heading *The Legislative Process*.

V. Tracking Federal Bills

Like Louisiana bill tracking, the Internet is the most convenient source for federal bill tracking. The Library of Congress's website provides a comprehensive resource, including bill summaries and status, committee reports, and the *Congressional Record*. Track a bill from the current Congress by running a search in the section marked *Legislation in Current Congress*. Search by key word(s) or by bill sponsor. Search bills from more than one Congress at a time by selecting *Search Multiple Congresses*, then selecting the sessions of Congress you would like to search. This feature is helpful if you are not sure of the exact session of Congress in which new legislation was enacted.

The *Congressional Record*, which is the official record of Congressional proceedings and debates, is also searchable through this website. Select a session of Congress and search the text of the *Congressional Record* with search terms, by date, or by member of Congress.

VI. Researching Federal Legislative History

Beyond looking to the plain meaning of a federal statute's words, court interpretations of the statute, and discussions of the statute in secondary sources, researching its legislative history may provide some guidance on its intent. Legislative history research requires the review of documents produced while a bill works its way through Congress. The primary documents worth reviewing include: (1) committee reports regarding the bill, (2) transcripts of floor debates on the bill, (3) minutes of hearings on the bill in committees and subcommittees, and (4) the original bill as it was introduced and its amendments.

Legislative history research can be done either in print or online. Notably, online databases are not all complete in terms of researching older statutes, so you should consider the coverage of an online source and the dates of the law you are checking to ensure that the source is compatible with your research task in terms of coverage.

Like the *2008 Compiled Edition of the Civil Codes of Louisiana* mentioned in Part III above, legislative histories of some federal statutes have already been compiled and published by others. If you are researching a well-known and influential piece of legislation, its legislative history may have already been compiled. Two references for compiled legislative histories are *Sources of Compiled Legislative Histories: A Bibliography of Government Documents, Periodical Articles, and Books* by Nancy P. Johnson and *Federal Legislative Histories: An Annotated Bibliography and Index to Officially Published Sources* by Bernard D. Reams, Jr.

If no legislative history has been compiled, several sources exist in which you may conduct your own legislative history.

Congressional Information Service (CIS) is the most comprehensive source for compiling legislative histories. It is available in print and electronically through LexisNexis Congressional. CIS indexes congressional materials going back as far as 1789.

To research in print, once you identify the relevant public law number, locate the CIS entry for the law in the CIS *Legislative Histories* volume.[6] The entry lists the legislative history documents for the law and provides a brief summary of each document. For each item in the list, the year of the document is indicated along with a CIS

---

6. Prior to 1984, *Legislative Histories* were listed in the CIS *Abstracts* volume, rather than published as a separate volume.

number, called an *accession number*, that identifies the corresponding microfiche containing the document. The microfiche records are organized by year, then by number. Notably, although CIS lists *Congressional Record* references, CIS microfiche records do not include *Congressional Record* documents, which must be obtained directly from the *Congressional Record*.

CIS also publishes *Index* volumes that can be searched by subject, law title or name, and bill number. An entry in the index references the *Abstracts* volume, which provides summaries of relevant documents and accession numbers linked to microfiche. CIS indexes and abstracts are updated monthly and annually.

Legislative histories prepared by CIS can also be researched electronically on LexisNexis Congressional. In addition to the references to legislative history documents noted above, the entries on this service are linked to the full text of many of the documents.

Another source for legislative history research is the *United States Code Congressional and Administrative News* (USCCAN). USCCAN is a West publication that provides laws, legislative history documents, presidential proclamations, executive orders, and other documents. The more recent volumes of USCCAN are divided into two sections: *Laws* and *Legislative History*, each of which is organized sequentially by public law number. The *Laws* section reprints the text of each public law as it appears in *Statutes at Large* and, if applicable, notes in the margins where the language has been codified in the United States Code. Following the text of each public law, USCCAN lists the more important elements of the law's legislative history, such as committee reports, the dates the law was considered and passed in each house of Congress, and any presidential statements regarding the law. The *Legislative History* section contains at least one committee report and the presidential signing statement, if available. USCCAN is not an exhaustive source of legislative history, but it can be a quick and easy way to find some of the basics. USCCAN is also available electronically on Westlaw.

The *Congressional Record* contains transcripts of Senate and House floor debates; however, legislators may revise and amend the transcripts, which means they may not accurately reflect actual floor debates. Documents in the *Congressional Record* are arranged in chronological order and can be found on microfiche in law libraries or on the Library of Congress's website. The Library of Congress's website, at http://thomas.loc.gov, provides the text of bills, congressional actions taken, public laws, bill summaries and status, and committee reports. You may search this site by public law number, by search terms in a database for a session or sessions of Congress, by bill sponsor, and by committee. This website also links to documents on the Government Printing Office website at www.access.gpo.gov.

Chapter 5

Judicial Systems
and Judicial Opinions

Judicial opinions are the written decisions of courts; they are also called cases. Not all judicial opinions are published outside of the court record of a case, but those that are published appear in print *reporters* and electronically on court databases and on services such as LexisNexis and Westlaw. Reporters are books in which the opinions of certain courts are published or in which opinions on a particular topic are published. As examples, the *United States Reports* is a reporter in which decisions written by the United States Supreme Court are published; the *Southern Reporter* publishes all state appellate court decisions from the courts of Louisiana, Mississippi, Alabama, and Florida; the series *Federal Rules Decisions* publishes cases decided by the federal district courts that address issues involving the Federal Rules of Civil Procedure and the Federal Rules of Criminal Procedure. The opinions published in reporters are usually published in chronological order.

The importance of researching judicial opinions is at least three-fold. First, prior judicial decisions will often be considered mandatory or binding authority to a court because those decisions are treated as law within the jurisdiction. Thus, the researcher is seeking statements of law when he is researching judicial opinions.[1] Second, even judicial decisions that are not considered to be mandatory authority are often quite persuasive and instructive to a court faced with

---

1. *See* Chapter 1, Part V (discussing the value of judicial decisions in Louisiana, in the federal courts, and in other states' courts).

a similar set of facts that must decide a legal issue similar to one previously decided by another court. And third, judicial decisions provide explanations and interpretations of the law that can help lawyers craft arguments and draw analogies or distinctions to advise clients on future actions and to argue to the court for a certain outcome.

With the easy access almost all lawyers and their staffs have to judicial decisions from courts of many jurisdictions, both in print and online, no lawyer should consider research complete until he has researched judicial opinions on an issue.

I. Judicial Systems

In the United States, most judicial or court systems, both state and federal, are primarily made up of three tiers of courts: (1) district or trial courts; (2) intermediate appellate courts; and (3) a supreme court or a state court of last resort. Court systems may also include some inferior or specialty courts, which are trial courts whose jurisdiction is restricted by subject matter or by maximum amount of recovery.

A. The Louisiana Judicial System

The Louisiana state judicial system includes judicial district courts, intermediate courts of appeal, and a supreme court. Louisiana also has a tier of inferior specialty courts. These inferior specialty courts are courts of *limited jurisdiction* because their jurisdiction or power to hear cases is restricted to certain subject matters or by a maximum amount in controversy. These inferior specialty courts include family courts, juvenile courts, traffic courts, city courts, parish courts, and mayor's courts. All other litigation will be filed in one of the judicial district courts, which are courts of *general jurisdiction* because their jurisdiction is not limited by subject matter or amount in controversy. See Figure 5-1 for a diagram of the Louisiana court structure. All judges in the Louisiana state court system are elected by the public.

Figure 5-1. Diagram of the Louisiana Court Structure

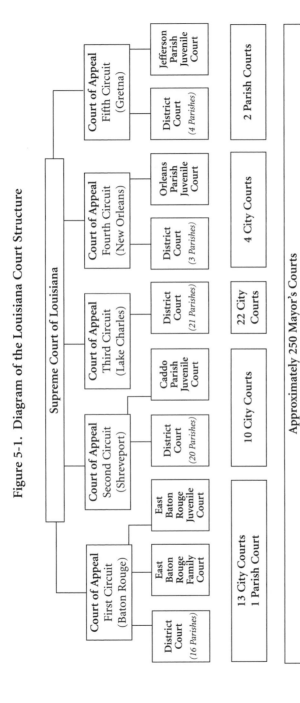

Source: *Annual Report 2006 of the Judicial Council of the Supreme Court of Louisiana.*

Louisiana has forty-two judicial districts. All numbered judicial district courts, from the First Judicial District to the Fortieth and the Forty-Second, hear both civil and criminal cases. The remaining judicial district is known as the Parish of Orleans; it is the forty-first judicial district, but it is seldom referenced by a numerial designation. Rather than having one court to hear civil, criminal, and juvenile cases, Orleans Parish has the Civil District Court for the Parish of Orleans, the Criminal District Court for the Parish of Orleans, and the Orleans Parish Juvenile Court. See Louisiana Lagniappe 5-1.

Louisiana Lagniappe 5-1.

Louisiana Parishes

In Louisiana, a *parish* is the designation used for what is referred to as a *county* in 48 other states in the United States. (Alaska uses the designation *borough* instead of county.) One or more parishes comprise each judicial district in Louisiana.

At the district court level, trials are held. If a trial is held, the parties will present evidence in the form of witnesses, documents, and objects. Both questions of fact and law are considered. The judge is responsible for deciding questions of law concerning the dispute between the parties. The judge or a jury is responsible for deciding questions of fact arising from the dispute between the parties. If a jury is seated to hear the case, the jury will render a *verdict*, which is its decision on the case. In a jury trial, the judge will enter a *judgment* on the verdict. If the case is tried to a judge without a jury, the court will render its own judgment.

Some issues may come before the court in the form of exceptions or motions made before, during, and sometimes after a trial. An *exception* is the name used in Louisiana for a motion filed with the court in which the litigant questions or takes issue with some aspect of the lawsuit, such as an exception to the court's jurisdiction over the case or a party or an exception to the timing of the filing of the suit.[2] Other *motions* may be made in which a litigant requests or moves the court to act, such as to dismiss a case.

---

2. The exceptions that may be brought in Louisiana are the declinatory, dilatory, and peremptory exceptions. La. Code Civ. Proc. Ann. arts. 921–23, 925–27 (2005 & Supp. 2013). The referenced articles identify some of the issues that may be addressed by filing an exception with the court.

The next level of state court is the intermediate appellate court. The courts at this level are referred to as the *Louisiana Courts of Appeal*. These courts consider appeals from final judgments of the district courts, judgments of family and juvenile courts, and certain administrative agency determinations. In extraordinary circumstances, these courts will consider appeals from decisions made by the district courts prior to a final judgment. The state is divided into five appellate circuits that have jurisdiction over appeals originating in the courts and sometimes agencies located within their circuits. Should an appeal be filed, a three-judge panel of an appellate court will consider the record of the district court's proceedings and the arguments of the parties, brought forth in written briefs and often through oral arguments. In almost all cases, the appellate courts will not consider any evidence or testimony that was not brought before the district court and made a part of the trial record.

In a civil case, an appellate court may review a decision on issues of fact and law. After review, the appellate court has the authority to affirm the district court's decision, reverse the decision and remand the case to the district court for further proceedings, or reverse the district court's decision and correct the errors that were made.[3] In a criminal case, the appellate court may review decisions only on issues of law.[4]

An appeal from a Louisiana Court of Appeal decision is to the Louisiana Supreme Court. *See* Louisiana Lagniappe 5-2. The Louisiana Supreme Court has *supervisory jurisdiction* over the decisions of the intermediate appellate courts. Supervisory jurisdiction means that the court has

Louisiana Lagniappe 5-2.
Louisiana Supreme Court
On March 1, 2013, the Louisiana Supreme Court celebrated 200 years as Louisiana's highest court. Louisiana Supreme Court Justice Bernette Joshua Johnson also became the first African American chief justice of the Court in 2013.

---

3. The power of the appellate court to review issues of fact as well as law and substitute its own judgment on these issues derives from Louisiana's civil law tradition. *Rosell v. ESCO*, 549 So. 2d 840, 844 & n.2 (La. 1989); La. Const. Ann. art. 5 § 10(B) (1996).

4. La. Const. Ann. art. 5 § 10(B).

the discretion, but not an obligation, to hear appeals from intermediate appellate court decisions. The court ordinarily hears appeals in fewer than 10% of the cases in which its supervisory jurisdiction is requested. The court also serves as the court of first appeal in certain cases. When a litigant appeals a decision in which a law or ordinance has been deemed unconstitutional, the litigant has a right to file its first appeal to the Supreme Court, bypassing the Court of Appeal. Additionally, a criminal defendant has a right of appeal to the Supreme Court when he has been found guilty of a capital offense and has been sentenced to death. Finally, the court has original jurisdiction in cases involving disciplinary actions against lawyers and judges. *Original jurisdiction* refers to the court sitting as a trial court on a case.

B. The Federal Judicial System and the Judicial Systems in Other States

The structure of the federal judicial system and most state judicial systems is similar to the Louisiana system described above. The federal judicial system includes district courts, intermediate appellate courts, and the United States Supreme Court. In addition to this basic structure, federal bankruptcy courts operate within almost every district to handle bankruptcy matters. The federal courts are courts of limited jurisdiction, which means that they only have the jurisdiction or power to hear certain cases. In general, cases within the federal court's jurisdiction are cases that arise under federal law and cases between citizens of different states with a sufficient amount in controversy.

The ninety-four federal district courts serve as the trial courts in the federal system. Like state trial courts, the federal district courts are the initial forum in which a case filed in the federal system is litigated. Bankruptcy courts within these districts will hear matters brought pursuant to federal bankruptcy laws. District court judges in the federal court system, as well as appellate court judges and Supreme Court justices, are appointed by the president and confirmed by the United States Senate. Bankruptcy court judges are appointed for fourteen-year terms by the federal appellate court judges. Federal magistrate judges, who assist the district court judges, are appointed by the district court judges to serve eight-year terms. Federal magistrate judges handle many pretrial matters in cases filed in the federal district courts, and they may serve as trial judges in civil and non-felony criminal cases with the consent of the parties.

Appeals of federal district court decisions are heard by the intermediate appellate court, which is the court of appeals for the particular circuit in which the trial court sits. Louisiana, Texas, and Mississippi sit within the jurisdiction of the Court of Appeals for the Fifth Circuit. When an appeal is filed, a three-judge panel of the court considers the record of the lower court's proceedings and the arguments of the parties. On issues of law, the appellate court will either affirm the lower court's decision, modify the decision, remand the case to the trial court for further proceedings, or reverse the lower court's decision and correct the errors that were made. On issues of fact, the appellate court will either affirm the lower court's decision or will reverse the decision and remand the case back to the lower court for a new trial or for further proceedings to correct the errors. The federal appellate court does not have the power to re-examine facts and substitute its own judgment on factual issues.

Once the appellate court renders its decision, if the litigants wish to appeal that decision they may seek an *en banc* review, which is a review by the entire appellate court, or they may seek review by the United States Supreme Court. The Supreme Court hears only a small fraction of the cases for which review is sought, which means that the appellate court is the court of last resort in most cases.

The Supreme Court is the highest court in the United States. Like the appellate court, the Supreme Court does not typically sit as a trial court, but it reviews the records from the proceedings of the lower courts. On issues of law, the Supreme Court will either affirm the lower court's decision or correct any errors that may have been made. On issues of fact, the Supreme Court will either affirm the district court's decision or will remand the case back to the district court for a new trial or for further proceedings to correct the errors found. In addition to hearing appeals from federal courts, the Supreme Court has the discretion to hear appeals from state high courts on issues of federal and constitutional law.

Most states have three-tier judicial systems that mirror the structures of the federal and Louisiana state systems, although court names differ among states. A minority of states do not have intermediate appellate courts.

II. Judicial Opinions

A. What To Expect in a Published Judicial Opinion

1. Courts' Opinions

When courts in the federal system and appellate courts in the state systems decide cases, they traditionally write opinions that summarize the facts of the cases, summarize the existing law, and explain how they have resolved the cases and why. Courts provide this information, in part, because they know that their opinions serve purposes beyond just explaining to the parties to the dispute how the case has been resolved. A judicial opinion in the United States not only resolves the dispute before the court, but it may also make law, provide readers with interpretations of the law that will be consulted in future analogous cases, and educate readers on the law. Notably, state trial court opinions are not widely published or disseminated in Louisiana and in most states. Additionally, in many jurisdictions around the world, lengthy opinions are not written.

A typical opinion written by a court in the United States for publication will include some or all of the following, though not necessarily in this order: (1) an introduction to the case in which the court may identify briefly the key facts and issues; (2) a statement of the case in which the court sets out the facts of the case and its procedural history; (3) a statement of the issues the court will address; (4) the applicable law, including enacted law and discussions of previously decided cases; (5) analysis of the case before the court or application of the law to the case before the court; and (6) the disposition of the case, which includes the court's resolution of the case and how that resolution affects any earlier dispositions by lower courts.

If the opinion is written by a majority of judges or justices sitting on a panel of judges, the court's opinion will be referred to as a *majority opinion*. A court's majority opinion is the only part of a published case that may be considered primary legal authority. A judge or judges who do not join in the majority's opinion might write a *concurring opinion* or a *dissenting opinion*. A concurring opinion or a concurrence is written by a judge or judges who agree with the majority's result, but for reasons different from the majority's opinion. A dissenting opinion is written by a judge or judges who disagree with the majority's result and reasoning. Another possibility is that an appellate court may write a *plurality opinion*, which is an opinion written by the largest number of judges on a court who agree to a result and reasoning, when that number of judges is fewer than a majority of the court.

For example, on a seven-person court like the Louisiana Supreme Court, four justices[5] might write a majority opinion, which is the official opinion of the court. Two justices may write a concurring opinion in which they state their agreement with the court's ruling, but state their disagreement with the court's reasoning and provide their own reasoning. A seventh justice may write a dissenting opinion in which he states his disagreement with the court's ruling and reasoning and provides his preferred result and reasoning. Judges are not required to write concurring or dissenting opinions.

Courts often include additional information in their opinions. The term *dicta* refers to information included in the court's opinion that is not necessary to support the court's decision. For example, a court may include a discussion of a hypothetical situation and how it might rule on that hypothetical. This information may be considered persuasive authority; it is never considered binding legal authority.

---

5. The term *judge* is used in this section to refer to the person or persons who preside over a judicial proceeding. Often, the term *justice* is used to refer to judges who sit on the highest court of a jurisdiction, such as is used here to refer to the justices of the Louisiana Supreme Court. You should determine the appropriate term to use to refer to the judges who sit on the courts in which you are working and researching.

2. Publishers' Research Aids

Publishers of reporters often include supplemental material to assist the researcher in reading and understanding opinions and to assist with further research of the issues discussed in opinions. This supplemental material is never considered legal authority, and *it should never be cited* as part of a court's opinion. For example, current decisions of the Louisiana Supreme Court are published in the *Southern Reporter, Third Series*. Figure 5-2 provides an excerpt from a judicial decision reported in the *Southern Third*, which is the term often used to refer to this reporter.

The publisher has added the case *docket number* before the title of the case, followed by a parenthetical that includes an abbreviation for the deciding court and the exact date on which the case was decided. The docket number is the number by which the case is identified by this court. This same information is repeated following the case name.

Then, the publisher has provided a *synopsis* or summary of the case and the court's holding and has identified the disposition of the case. These sections, as well as the headnotes that follow them, are most often written by the publisher's editorial staff; they are typically not authoritative. The summary is a good place to start to determine whether to choose the case for further research.

The *headnotes* are also helpful in this task. The headnotes are numbered paragraphs in which the publisher has identified key points of law discussed in the decision. These numbers correspond to bracketed and bold numbers added by the publisher to the text of the opinion, which identify where those points are discussed by the court. Legal researchers and writers should avoid the temptation to cite to or quote the headnotes because they are not part of the court's opinion. Instead, the researcher should use the headnotes as a guide to the points discussed by the court in the opinion. The headnotes also include references to topics and key numbers from the West digest system, which are discussed in Chapter 6.

Other features found in the *Southern Third* publication of a case include the names of the attorneys and who they represent. This in-

Figure 5-2. Case Excerpt

2012-0239 (La. 10/16/12)
Jade BOUDREAUX

v.

LOUISIANA DEPARTMENT OF PUBLIC SAFETY
AND CORRECTIONS.

No. 2012-C-0239

Supreme Court of Louisiana
Oct. 16, 2012.

Background: Following acquittal on second charge of driving while intoxicated (DWI), driver filed rule to show cause why his license should not be immediately reinstated. Office of Motor Vehicles (OMV) sought restriction on reinstatement. The 19th Judicial District Court, East Baton Rouge Parish, granted reinstatement without restriction. The Court of Appeal, First Circuit, 80 So. 3d 767, affirmed. OMV sought writ review.

Holdings: The Supreme Court, Knoll, J., granted writ and held that:
(1) arrest and charge of an individual for an alleged violation of the DWI statute are not sufficient to constitute an actual "violation" of the DWI statute;
(2) driver's second arrest on charge of DWI, without more, did not constitute second violation of the DWI statute; and
(3) driver was entitled to reinstatement of his license without restriction.

Affirmed.
Johnson, J., dissented.
Guidry, J., concurred in the result and assigned reasons.

1. Statutes ⌾ 181(1)

In all cases of statutory interpretation, legislative intent is the fundamental question, and the well-established rules of statutory construction are designed to ascertain and enforce the intent of the statute.

Source: *Boudreaux v. La. Dep't of Pub. Safety & Corrs.*, 101 So. 3d 22 (La. 2012). Reprinted with permission of Thomson Reuters.

formation is placed after the headnotes. Another feature is perpendicular lines with a number on them, which are interspersed throughout the opinion. This feature provides the page numbers of the court's original opinion, which are necessary for a public domain citation to the case.

B. Louisiana Judicial Opinions

1. The Importance of Louisiana Judicial Opinions

> **Louisiana Lagniappe 5-3.**
>
> **The Value of Cases**
>
> Explaining the theory behind valuing judicial opinions, but not requiring strict adherence to opinions as a source of law, Professor Ferdinand Stone wrote: "There is much wisdom in the reports, much useful analogy, much experience, but even so, we must remember that neither wisdom nor experience is the monopoly of any one age or of any one set of judges. The search for truth and justice must be a continual search, a building from the truth and error of the past to the solution of the present and the hope for the future." Ferdinand Stone, *Tort Doctrine in Louisiana*, 17 Tul. L. Rev. 159, 214 (1942), *quoted in Ardoin v. Hartford Accident & Indem. Co.*, 360 So. 2d 1331, 1334 n.7 (1978).

As is discussed in more detail in Part V of Chapter 1, there is some question in Louisiana as to whether judicial opinions by Louisiana state courts are considered a source of law. According to the Louisiana Civil Code, some Louisiana Supreme Court decisions, and the civil law tradition, judicial opinions may provide examples of how the law should be interpreted and applied, but they are not a source of law.[6] Applying the doctrine of *jurisprudence constante*, a long line of consistent decisions may carry great weight as to how to interpret the law, but it would not bind a court. See Louisiana Lagniappe 5-3. In practice, prior opinions are usually highly val-

---

6. La. Civ. Code Ann. art. 1 (1999); *Doerr v. Mobil Oil Corp.*, 774 So. 2d 119, 128 (La. 2000) (explaining that "[j]udicial decisions ... are not intended to be an authoritative source of law in Louisiana"); *Ardoin v. Hartford Accident & Indem. Co.*, 360 So. 2d 1331, 1334 (La. 1978) (explaining that the "case law" provides a valuable interpretation of enacted law, "but it is nevertheless secondary information").

ued and in many instances are considered binding by trial and intermediate appellate courts when the court that rendered the prior decision is the court that may review the new decision.

The significance of this practice is that the researcher of Louisiana law should always search for enacted law that might govern a legal issue, but should also look for judicial interpretations of that law. More frequently than not, enacted law will provide the starting point for a Louisiana court's legal analysis, but the Louisiana court will almost always consider judicial opinions in which that enacted law has been interpreted.

Thus, Louisiana Supreme Court opinions are highly respected and are almost always followed by all Louisiana courts. Louisiana intermediate appellate court opinions are not a source of law. However, Louisiana district courts show great respect for appellate court opinions, especially when the opinions are rendered by the appellate court to which their decisions will be appealed. Further, Louisiana appellate courts and the Louisiana Supreme Court consider these appellate court opinions persuasive when they interpret the law.

2. Reporting of Louisiana Judicial Opinions

Louisiana Supreme Court opinions are published on the Louisiana Supreme Court's website, www.lasc.org, as soon as they are completed and released. Opinions may be accessed on the Supreme Court's website if they were released by the court in 1996 or after. To access an opinion through the website, you must know the date of the opinion's release. A tab across the top of the website is titled *News Releases*. Clicking on this tab opens up a new window and allows you to choose the release date of the opinion you are seeking, then click on the opinion. In terms of researching judicial opinions, the website does not provide an effective means of conducting new research, although it is helpful for simply locating opinions for which you have a release date available. Additionally, these opinions do not include publisher add-ons, like topic and key number references and headnotes.

Louisiana Supreme Court opinions are also published in the *Southern Reporter,* the *Southern Reporter, Second Series,* and the

Southern Reporter, Third Series, which can be located in their print versions as well as on online services such as Westlaw and LexisNexis. Opinions have been published in the *Southern Reporter* series since November 1886. The opinions first appear in *advance sheets* of the *Southern Reporter* series. Advance sheets are softbound, printed volumes that are published before the hardbound reporters are published. Supreme Court opinions are arranged chronologically in advance sheets followed by the opinions of the Louisiana Courts of Appeal. The advance sheets bear the volumes and page numbers that correspond to the later published hardbound reporters. In addition to opinions, the advance sheets include other features, including an alphabetical list of cases reported in the volume and a topic and key number digest for the cases reported in the volume. See Chapter 6 on using a digest.

Opinions of the Louisiana Courts of Appeal are published on each court's website as soon as they are released. They are also published in the *Southern Reporter,* the *Southern Reporter, Second Series,* and the *Southern Reporter, Third Series,* where they have appeared since 1928. *Southern Third* first publishes the opinions in an advance sheet following the Louisiana Supreme Court decisions, before including opinions in a hardbound volume.

The appellate courts' websites allow the researcher to locate opinions by the date the opinion was handed down. Additionally, the First Circuit Court of Appeal's website allows the searching of cases by key words, and the Fourth Circuit Court of Appeal's website allows searching by names of litigants and case number. These websites do not provide access to decisions handed down before 1997, and some do not go that far back. The website addresses for the various courts may be found in Appendix B, which includes websites of interest in Louisiana.

Louisiana district court opinions, like most state district court opinions, are not published commercially. They are usually provided only to the parties involved in the litigation.

C. Federal Judicial Opinions and Opinions of Other State Courts

While the *Southern Reporter* series publishes Louisiana *state* court decisions, decisions rendered by *federal* courts are found in different sets of reporters, even when the federal courts sit within the state of Louisiana. Table 5-1 provides a listing of the courts within the federal court system and the reporters in which their decisions are reported, with their proper citation abbreviations.

Table 5-1. Reporters for Federal Court Cases

Court	Reporter Name	Abbreviation
U.S. Supreme Court	*United States Reports* (official reporter)	U.S.
	Supreme Court Reporter	S. Ct.
	United States Supreme Court Reports, Lawyers' Edition	L. Ed. or L. Ed. 2d
U.S. Courts of Appeal	*Federal Reporter*	F. or F.2d or F.3d
	Federal Appendix	F. App'x
U.S. District Courts	*Federal Supplement*	F. Supp. or F. Supp. 2d
	Federal Rules Decisions (restricted to procedural issues)	F.R.D.

United States Supreme Court decisions are published in many places, both electronic and in print. Electronically they are published on several websites at no charge, including the following:

- The Supreme Court's website, at www.supremecourtus.gov
- FindLaw, at www.findlaw.com/casecode/supreme.html
- Oyez, at www.oyez.org
- Cornell's Legal Information Institute website, at www.law.cornell.edu/supct/index.html
- FedWorld (a program of the Commerce Department), at http://supcourt.ntis.gov.

Opinions are also available for a fee on the Westlaw and LexisNexis electronic databases and for free on databases such as Google Scholar.

In print, a researcher will find Supreme Court opinions in the *United States Reports*, the *Supreme Court Reporter*, the *United States Supreme Court Reports, Lawyers' Edition*, and *United States Law Week*. The official reporter of these opinions is the *United States Reports*, but its publication is years behind the release dates of the opinions. If a decision has not yet appeared in the *United States Reports*, cite to the *Supreme Court Reporter*, if the decision appears there. Decisions of the United States Courts of Appeals are published on the appellate court websites as well as in print in the *Federal Reporter* series, which includes the *Federal Reporter*, the *Federal Reporter, Second*, and the *Federal Reporter, Third*. These decisions are also published on the FindLaw website and the Cornell website noted above, as well as on Westlaw and LexisNexis. Some decisions of the courts of appeals are designated by the courts as *not for publication*. This designation usually strips the case of some or all of its precedential value, depending on the particular court's rules. The *Federal Appendix* is a reporter in which many of these cases are published. Additionally, some of these cases are available on Westlaw and LexisNexis.

Many federal district court decisions are published in print in the *Federal Supplement* reporter, which also has a second series, *Federal Supplement, Second*. District court decisions addressing issues involving the Federal Rules of Civil Procedure or the Federal Rules of Criminal Procedure may be published in the *Federal Rules Decisions* reporter, instead of the *Federal Supplement*. Electronically, these opinions are published on individual court websites and on both free and fee-based websites.

The state court decisions of courts in state systems other than Louisiana are published in either regional reporters, which include the decisions rendered by the courts of several states, like the *Southern Reporter*, or in state specific reporters. A simple way to determine in which publication a particular state court's decisions are published is to check Table 1 in *The Bluebook* or Appendix A in the *ALWD Citation Manual*. Both of these sources provide reporter names by jurisdiction and proper abbreviations for the reporters.

III. Reading and Analyzing Judicial Opinions or Cases

Armed with the knowledge of what components you may find when reading a case, you should recognize that reading and understanding cases may be more difficult and time-consuming than expected, especially when you are first starting out. Cases, especially older ones, may include *legalese* that interrupts a smooth reading and interferes with comprehension. Words such as *said, heretofore, aforementioned*, and *hereinafter* can be distracting.

The use of legal terms that are not familiar to you may also slow you down and require you to consult a legal dictionary. Understanding these terms is usually critical to understanding a case, so take the time to gather the necessary information. Courts may refer to parties by name or they may refer to parties by their roles in the case, such as *plaintiff* and *defendant, appellant* and *appellee, petitioner* and *respondent*. Courts may dispose of cases after a trial on the merits, in which case the courts may reference a jury *verdict* or a court's *judgment*. However, many times courts dispose of cases before a trial, such as by *summary judgment* or *default judgment*, or based on a post-trial motion, such as a *motion for judgment as a matter of law*. Appellate courts might sit *en banc* or they might hear a case after granting a *writ of mandamus*. Legal dictionaries are available in print and online. You should consult them whenever you come upon an unfamiliar word.

Finally, you should have a plan or system in place for evaluating and keeping track of cases. This advice applies to all research sources, but it will be discussed here as it applies to cases. Upon identifying cases as you research, work through these five steps for each case, unless and until you discard a case because it is not relevant: (1) skim; (2) read; (3) brief; (4) categorize; and (5) update.

A. Skim

When you first identify a list of potentially relevant cases, skim the syllabus or the synopsis of each case and its headnotes to determine if the case is worth a more careful read. You might also skim the first paragraph of the opinion and the portions of the opinion that correspond to the headnotes relevant to your issue. Consider whether the case has facts that are similar to your facts and whether it addresses legal issues that are similar to the legal issues you are facing. When you are looking at factual similarities, your focus should be on *legally significant facts* (*i.e.*, those facts that were relevant to the court's decision in the case).

You should include cases that support your position, if you have a position, as well as cases that do not. A thorough legal evaluation includes a consideration of both favorable and unfavorable decisions. Moreover, when arguing a position to a court, attorneys are bound by ethics rules to present controlling cases on point that are contrary to their positions.

When in doubt about a case's relevance at this stage, either skim through more of the case before making your decision or include the case for a more careful read. Then copy or print those cases that you have identified. Be sure to note on your list of cases the result of your evaluation of each case so that you do not repeat this step unnecessarily.

B. Read

Once you have identified cases through skimming parts of the cases, go back to those cases you have chosen for a more careful read. Skim the entire case, but read carefully those parts of the case that are relevant to the issue or issues you are researching. Many researchers highlight or jot down margin notes at this stage, identifying key passages in the case, such as the court's holding, critical facts, or well-stated rules.

As you read, make sure you identify and understand the parties and their roles, the legally significant facts, the court's holding and reasoning on the issue or issues in which you are interested, the rules the court is applying to the facts, and any policies or equitable principles that may be driving the court's decision. These are all items you will include in a brief of the case. Additionally, you may begin to categorize cases at this point based on what issue or issues they address. Jot down categories as you read.

You might also determine that a case is not helpful. Record your decision on your list of citations and file the case with other sources that have turned out not to be helpful. Do not discard these sources just yet because as you learn more about the law you might reconsider their usefulness.

C. Brief

Briefing is a way to take notes on a case. Typically, briefs include information organized by categories, which may vary by researcher and may vary by type of project. Students briefing cases for a particular class may use categories recommended by a professor or stressed by a professor through questioning. For example, briefs for a civil procedure class will typically include a procedural history section documenting the path the case has taken to get to the deciding court and they will focus on the procedural issues discussed by the court. These briefs will be used to assist the student in discussing the case in class and to assist the student in preparing for exams.

On the other hand, researchers writing briefs should focus briefs on the issues pertinent to their research, even if the cases include other issues. Researchers might also limit the information they include to what they will need to analyze the issue and write up their analysis.

Some researchers will skip the briefing step and will highlight and write more detailed notes on their case copies during the reading step. A researcher who chooses this approach should make sure that he fully understands the information that he is highlighting or marking in cases. Briefing requires the researcher to interact more with the information than does simply reading, helping to ensure a better understanding. For example, it is fairly simple to drag a highlighter across words representing the court's holding without carefully reading those words; briefing will prompt the researcher to read the words more carefully to make sense of them before paraphrasing them in a brief or even writing them verbatim.

For whatever purpose the brief is being written, below are some categories that will help to organize notes on a case.

Heading. Include the name of the case, the court, the exact date the case was decided, and the citation for the case (volume, reporter, and first page). Be sure to include all information necessary for properly citing the case so that you will not have to backtrack to gather information. You may also include a unique word or phrase about the case to identify it to you, such as *dog bite case* or *spice contract case.* Once you begin to categorize cases based on the points you want to make or the issues they address, you might also include the category here as well.

Issue or Issues. Identify the question or questions addressed by the court that are pertinent to your research.

Facts. Include legally significant facts and necessary background facts. If emotional facts appear to have played a role in the court's decision, include those as well.

Holding and Reasoning. Identify the court's response to the issue or question presented by the case and the reason for that response. The reasoning provides the analysis behind the court's holding. Thus, the holding might be, "Yes, the contract was binding," and the reasoning will include the reason or the "why" behind that holding.

Rules. Identify the rules, principles, and policies the court applied to the facts to reach its holding. This section may overlap with the reasoning, but unlike the reasoning it will be set forth in more general terms, not tied to the facts of the particular case. It may include a statute, it may include a principle from a prior case, and it may include a public policy or an equitable principle.

Other. Use this section to jot down notes about how this case will work for or against you and why it is significant. For example, identify how this case fits with your other cases or statutes or rules. It might modify or change or further interpret the law. Identify points on which this case is particularly helpful or harmful to the legal issue in your case. The court may have stated the law particularly well or explained the meaning of a term. The case may be a good case to compare to your case on a point or you might decide that you must distinguish the case from your case.

D. Categorize

Although this step is listed fourth, the researcher should always work with an eye toward imposing order on his research and on the final product of his research, whether it is a memorandum, a brief, a client letter, an oral report, or some other result. Categories for sorting cases might be based on such things as (1) the elements of a tort or a particular cause of action, (2) the requirements for a valid contract, (3) a majority and a minority view in an area of law, or (4) one jurisdiction's law versus another. Some cases might fall into more than one category. You may decide to outline the project by category and list the cases that are helpful next to each category in the outline. You may decide to physically stack cases by category. You may use a numbering system or a color coding system to categorize with a number or color associated with specific categories.

All of these suggestions represent ways to keep track of what you have found. When you know what you have and how it fits with the law and with your other sources, you will have a better sense of what you may still need to gather and when you have finished gathering. The next step, updating cases, is also critical to evaluating research progress and determining when research is complete.

E. Update

Updating, which is also referred to as *Sheparding*[7] and *Key-Citing*,[8] refers to checking the cases and other sources you have found (1) to make sure that they are still good law or valid statements about the current law, and (2) to find additional sources that have cited them. The updating services mentioned provide you with the prior and subsequent *history* of the case you are checking, they collect citations to cases and some secondary sources in which the cited authority has been mentioned, and they provide some indication about how these new sources have treated the cited authority.

Updating cases is essential to ensure thorough and accurate research. Be sure to incorporate this step into your process of reading and analyzing cases, and be sure to keep track of when you perform this step by marking your cases, your briefs, or your master citation list.

How to update cases is discussed further in Chapters 6 and 8.

---

7. *Shepardizing* refers to using *Shepard's Citations*, either in print or online through LexisNexis, to update citations.

8. *KeyCiting* refers to using the KeyCite feature on the online Westlaw service to update citations.

Chapter 6

Researching Judicial Opinions: Digests and Other Finding Tools and Strategies

This chapter discusses the digest and other tools and strategies to effectively locate relevant judicial opinions in print and online. An effective researcher will consider where to begin research based on the following: (1) what information the researcher already has, (2) what resources are available, and (3) what sources will provide the most direct and expeditious route to the information sought.

I. Beginning with a Citation to a Relevant Statute

You may know that enacted law—a particular statute, article, or rule—governs a legal issue. If so, locate the annotated version of the enacted law, either in print or online. The section of the annotation labeled as *Notes of Decisions* will include brief summaries of the legal issues discussed in cases in which the enacted law has been cited and it will provide citations to the cases. If working in the print version of the enacted law, be sure to check any pocket parts or supplements for the most recent annotations. Collect the citations to the cases that sound most relevant and either pull the appropriate volumes of the reporters to locate the cases or type in the case citations online to view the cases. As is discussed in Chapter 5, most cases may be located online on free websites and on fee-paid services.

After identifying relevant cases, use those cases to find additional cases by one of the methods set forth in the next section. Then, *update* the cases, as explained below and in Chapter 8.

II. Beginning with a Citation to a Relevant Case[1]

You may be given a citation to a relevant case and be expected to fully research the issue beyond the one case. In that circumstance, locate the relevant case in print or online and review it. If it proves helpful, search for additional, relevant cases by: (1) retrieving the cases cited by the court in the relevant case that addresses the issue; (2) updating the relevant case using a citator service; and (3) using the headnotes in the case to identify topics and key numbers for use in the appropriate digest. The first of these methods needs no further explanation. The second and third methods are discussed below.

A. Updating to Find Additional Cases

As was mentioned in Chapter 5, updating refers to checking the citations of cases and other sources both to make sure that they are still good law or valid statements about the current law and to find additional sources that have cited them. Updating using a citator service not only provides you with the prior and subsequent history of the case you are checking, but also provides a list of citations to cases, some secondary sources, and court documents in which the cited source has been mentioned and indicates how these new sources have treated the cited source. The case being updated is referred to as the *cited source*; the sources in which the cited source has been cited are referred to as *citing sources*.

---

1. See Section III.D below for a discussion on where to begin when you have been given the name of one or both of the parties to a potentially relevant case without a case citation.

The most efficient and effective place to update is online, using either Westlaw's KeyCite feature or LexisNexis's Shepard's feature.[2] Once you click on either of these features, you will be prompted to enter the citation of the case you are checking. You will then be given a list of citations to sources.

Those cases listed under *history* are the prior and subsequent history of the cited source or case; that is, they involve the same parties and the same or related litigation between those parties. History will include citations to dispositions of the cited case, such as *writ granted, writ denied, affirmed, modified,* and *reversed.*

Those cases listed under *citing references* or *citing decisions* mention specifically the case you are checking. This list is your potential source of additional, relevant cases for your research. This list is also referred to as the *treatment* of the cited source. In addition to the citations, the Shepard's or KeyCite entries indicate the type of treatment of the cited case by the citing source. Shepard's uses signals and words to indicate the treatment of a case, such as a red stop sign to indicate negative treatment or the words *followed by* to show that the citing source has followed the cited source. KeyCite on Westlaw lists negative references first followed by positive references. It also indicates the depth of treatment of a cited case by using a star system, with one star indicating just a mention of the case up to four stars indicating an examination of the case.

You may click on the citing sources one at a time to see if they are helpful to you or you may print the citation list and locate the sources in print in reporters. Which one of these options you choose may depend on the terms of your fee schedule with the service. If you have free access to these services, accessing the cases online is probably the most efficient use of your time. Moreover, even if you are being charged to use the service, you may save time and money by quickly skimming the cases on the list online to determine which

2. *Shepard's Citators* are also published in print, but the print versions are not as up to date as their online counterparts. *Shepard's Citators* are discussed in Chapter 8.

ones are worth a more careful read and which ones are not helpful. Then, you may either print those cases or pull just those cases in the reporters.

B. Using Headnotes from One Case to Find Additional Cases

An additional way to use a relevant case to find additional cases is to use the topics and key numbers associated with the headnotes from your relevant case in the proper West digest or online on Westlaw. Each of the headnotes that precedes the court's opinion in a West reporter, such as the *Southern Second* reporter, is tied to a topic and key number in the West digest system. The digest collects cases that address the particular legal issue under that same topic and key number, allowing you access to citations to additional cases on that point.

What this means is that once you find a relevant case, you may use the topics and key numbers that correspond to the relevant points of law in which you are interested in any digest in the West system to find additional cases. Sometimes the initial case is from the jurisdiction in which you are researching. Thus, if you research Louisiana law and locate a Louisiana case in which Louisiana law is applied, you may use the topics and key numbers from that case in the *Louisiana Digest 2d* to find additional cases. At other times, the initial case is from a jurisdiction other than the one you are researching or the court in that case is applying the law of a different jurisdiction. You may still use the topics and key numbers from that case in the relevant digest to locate cases on the same legal point from your jurisdiction.

For example, if the researcher of Louisiana law learns of a case decided by a Florida state court applying Florida law that is on the same point of law he is researching, he may use the topics and key numbers from that Florida case in the *Louisiana Digest* to find Louisiana cases on the point. West uses the same topics and key numbers in all of its reporters and digests, which makes research information gained from one jurisdiction transferrable to other jurisdictions' digests.

See Figure 6-1 for examples of entries from the *Louisiana Digest 2d* and the *Florida Digest 2d* under the same topic and key number: topic Homicide, key number 540. Note that the same point of law is being discussed in the different digests.

Figure 6-1. Digest Excerpts

Excerpt from the *Florida Digest 2d*, Homicide 540—In general.	Excerpt from the *Louisiana Digest 2d*, Homicide 540—In general.
Fla. 2002. Evidence was sufficient to support defendant's convictions of first-degree murder with a deadly weapon and armed kidnaping with a weapon; defendant and two accomplices knocked victim unconscious with baseball bat in victim's home, took victim to nearby wooded area, secured him to a tree, and beat, stabbed, and slashed him repeatedly over period of several days, setting his body on fire after his death. West's F.S.A. §921.141(4).—Bell v. State, 841 So.2d 329, rehearing denied.	**La. 1993.** To prove crime of first-degree murder through killing an individual with intent to kill or inflict great bodily harm upon more than one person, state was required to prove two elements: defendant killed victim and defendant had specific intent to kill or to inflict great bodily harm upon more than one person. LSA-R.S. 14:30, subd. A(3). State v. Bourque, 622 So.2d 198, appeal after remand 699 So.2d 1, 1996-0842 (La. 7/1/97), rehearing denied, certiorari denied 118 S.Ct. 1514, 523 U.S. 1073, 140 L.Ed.2d 667.

Sources: *Florida Digest 2d* and *Louisiana Digest 2d 2008 cumulative annual pocket parts*. Reprinted with permission of Thomson Reuters.

Similarly, you may use the topics and key numbers from a relevant case on Westlaw to find additional relevant cases. Once you have found a case that is relevant to your legal issue, you may click on the pertinent topic and key number listed with the headnote in that case to identify a listing of additional cases in which that same point of law has been discussed.

III. Using the West Digest System to Begin Research or to Continue Research

Using a digest is one of the most efficient ways to locate citations to cases on the issues you are researching. A digest is a multi-volume set of books that organizes *annotations* (summaries of legal issues from cases) by topics and provides you with citations to the cases. See Figure 6-1. Think of the digest as an especially thorough index to the cases.

> **Louisiana Lagniappe 6-1.**
>
> ### Digest of 1808
>
> In 2008, Louisiana celebrated the 200th anniversary of the publication of *A Digest of the Civil Laws Now in Force in the Territory of Orleans*. This document is also known as the *Digest of 1808*. It was written as an attempt to codify the laws in force in Louisiana, which at the time included Spanish law, French law, and American law. The *Digest of 1808* was written in French and translated into English. This use of the term *digest* should not be confused with the digest described in this chapter.

While reporters organize cases chronologically, digests are organized by topic. (See Louisiana Lagniappe 6-1 for a different use of the word *digest* in Louisiana.)

West publishes many different reporters that together contain decisions from all state appellate courts and all federal courts, and it publishes digests to provide access to these decisions. The discussion following focuses on the features of West digests. Digests published by other publishers will have some of these same features. Once aware of the various features of the digest, you will be able to choose the best entry point into the digest system to collect citations to relevant cases. For example, the previous section discussed the best entry point into the digest when you already have a relevant case and are looking to find additional cases.

A. Feature 1: Organization by Topics

West digests are organized by *topics*. Currently, there are more than 400 topics into which the legal points made in cases are organized.

These topics fit under one of seven main divisions of law identified by West as Persons, Property, Contracts, Torts, Crimes, Remedies, and Government. A listing of these seven main divisions with the topics related to each is found in the front of each volume of each digest under the heading *Outline of the Law*. Additionally, an alphabetical, numbered list of topics is included in the front of each volume of each digest. The numbers are not particularly useful to the researcher in the print digest, but the numbers may be used in searches on Westlaw, which is discussed below.

Volumes of the digest are arranged alphabetically by topic, with the first and last topics included in a particular volume listed on the spine of the volume. Some topics, such as *Criminal Law*, span the text of many volumes of the digest. Other topics, such as *Dead Bodies*, span only a handful of pages within one volume of the digest. If you already know under which topic your legal issue fits, you may go straight to that topic in the digest.

Topics are broken down even further into subtopics, which are identified by numbers called *key numbers* because of the figure of a key that precedes them. At the beginning of each topic, a statement of the *subjects included* under the topic and the *subjects excluded* is provided, as are cross references to other related topics. Additionally, a topical analysis precedes the annotations. The *analysis* is organized like a table of contents, identifying the subtopics and their respective key numbers. The analysis is essential to the researcher who is researching a topic such as Criminal Law that spans multiple volumes of the digest.

Following this prefatory material are the annotations, which are arranged within the subtopics by court and date. The annotations include a court abbreviation, the year in which the case was decided, a summary of the legal issue from the case, the case name, and the case citation. The summaries match the information that is found in the headnotes that precede the courts' opinions in West publications of cases. Thus, the topic and key number associated with a headnote in a case provide an address to where the researcher might find additional cases on that legal issue in the digest.

The annotations are not the law and should never be cited as authority. Use the annotations to identify relevant cases for your review. If the cases prove to be helpful, cite the cases.

West digests are updated through the use of pocket parts and supplements and through the inclusion of a list of topics and key numbers in the front of each advance sheet of the West reporters. Thus, each of these sources should be consulted to ensure a thorough digest search.

For example, if a researcher were researching the elements of first-degree murder, he might begin by looking at the West Outline of the Law, which is found in the front of any West digest volume, under the heading *Crimes*, where he would find that *Homicide* is a digest topic. He could then pull the digest volume that includes the topic *Homicide* and scan the topic analysis for subtopics and key numbers that appear to be relevant. He would then turn to those subtopics and key numbers in both the main volume of the digest and any pocket parts or supplements and read the annotations to locate citations to relevant cases. He would make a list of potential case citations, locate those cases either in print reporters or online, and read the cases to determine their relevancy. For those cases that he deems relevant and helpful, he would update them to make sure that they are valid statements of the law.

B. Feature 2: The Descriptive-Word Index

Sometimes you will not be familiar with an area of law and will not be able to choose a topic in which to begin research. Sometimes the research issue will seem to fall within several digest topics. Sometimes the topic will have so many subtopics that you will want more specific direction.

In any of these circumstances, the *Descriptive-Word Index* is the best entry point into the digest. It is an index that spans several volumes near the end of the digest set. After generating search terms, as is discussed in Chapter 2, Section I.B, use those terms in the Descriptive-Word Index to identify potential, relevant topics and key numbers. The Descriptive-Word Index does not provide case citations. Rather, it directs the researcher to topics and key numbers. The index is updated with pocket parts and supplements.

For example, the researcher who is trying to identify the elements of first-degree murder under Louisiana law might turn to the Descriptive-Word Index of the *Louisiana Digest 2d*, rather than turning to a digest topic. If he uses the Descriptive-Word Index and looks up the term *murder* in the main volume, he finds the following entry: "See heading **HOMICIDE**, generally." If he checks the pocket part to that same volume and looks up the term *murder*, however, he is not only cross referenced to homicide, but he will also find an entire listing of subheadings and references to topics and key numbers relevant to murder.[3] He will use his other search terms within this entry to focus in more particularly on the issue he is researching. When he looks up the term *first-degree murder* within the murder section of the pocket part, he will find several references to various subtopics and he will find references to various key numbers under the topic Homicide. See Figure 6-2 for an excerpt from the Descriptive-Word Index of this section. He will make a list of the topics and key numbers that seem most relevant and will pull those corresponding volumes of the digest to locate annotations.

Notably, had the researcher begun his research with the search term *homicide* or with some other relevant term, he would have been referred to the same set of topics and key numbers and he would have been cross referenced to the terms *murder* and *homicide* within the index.

As in using any type of index, the researcher who tries his search terms and is unsuccessful should brainstorm even further to develop additional terms. Suggestions for doing this are set forth in Chapter 2.

C. Feature 3: Words and Phrases

When researchers are looking for the basic definition of a legal term, they typically consult a legal dictionary. Legal dictionaries, like

---

3. Research tip: always check the pocket part first in any research source so that you will see the most up-to-date information first. You can then go to the main volume to gather additional information, if necessary.

Figure 6-2. Excerpt from the Descriptive-Word Index

References are to Digest Topics and Key Numbers	

MURDER
See also heading HOMICIDE,
    generally
FIRST degree murder,
    Generally, **Homic 540**
Atrocity,
    Weight and sufficiency of
      evidence, **Homic 1144**
Attempted murder, **Homic 561(2)**
Circumstantial evidence,
    weight and sufficiency,
    Homic 1140
Cruelty,
    Weight and sufficiency of
      evidence, **Homic 1144**
	MURDER—Cont'd
	    Deliberation and premeditation,
	    Homic 542
	    Sufficiency and time
	      required, **Homic 543**
	    Weight and sufficiency of
	      evidence, **Homic 1143**
	    Evidence,
	      Weight and sufficiency.
	      See Weight and suffi-
	      ciency of evidence, post.
	    Instructions, **Homic 1377**
	    Instrument or device used,
	      nature of,
	      Weight and sufficiency of
	      evidence, **Homic 1145**

Source: *West's Louisiana Digest 2d 2008 cumulative annual pocket part.* Reprinted with permission of Thomson Reuters.

other types of dictionaries, provide general definitions of words and terms. However, when a researcher needs to identify the definition of a particular legal term according to the courts of a particular jurisdiction or the courts within a particular court system, the *Words and Phrases* section of the digest is the place to start.

Words and Phrases is a section or feature of the digest with an alphabetical listing of legal terms. You can browse the list to locate judicial definitions of terms, which are accompanied by the court, date, case name, and case citation of the case in which the term was defined. Also included is the relevant headnote that corresponds to the court's discussion of the term, a listing of relevant topics and key numbers, and identification of any relevant enacted law referenced by the court. See Figure 6-3 for an example of an entry from Words and Phrases.

Figure 6-3. Excerpt from Words and Phrases

COMPONENT PARTS

La. 2001. Gaming equipment, which could be removed from riverboat gaming vessel without substantial damage to the equipment or the vessel, did not constitute "component parts" of riverboat gaming vessel within meaning of sales tax exemption for component parts of a vessel; removing slot machines involved merely unplugging power cord, undoing three or four bolts, and lifting the machine, and slot machines were regularly moved to maintain customer interest. LSA–C.C. art. 466; LSA–R.S. 47:305.1, subd. A.—Showboat Star Partnership v. Slaughter, 789 So.2d 554, 2000-1227 (La. 4/3/01), rehearing denied.— Tax 3656.

Source: *West's Louisiana Digest 2d 2008 cumulative annual pocket part.* Reprinted with permission of Thomson Reuters.

The cases identified using Words and Phrases would also be identified through a search using the Descriptive-Word Index. However, Words and Phrases specifically focuses the researcher only on those cases in which the particular term has been interpreted and defined, while the Descriptive-Word Index will include a broader set of cases.

Words and Phrases volumes are updated using pocket parts and supplemental volumes and through the inclusion of a Words and Phrases section in the front of each advance sheet of the West reporters.

D. Feature 4: Table of Cases

The *Table of Cases* is a helpful tool to locate a case when you have learned the name of one or both of the parties to a case, but do not have a citation to the case. It is also another entry point into the digest because each case entry includes a list of topics and key numbers for the legal issues raised in the case.

The Table of Cases is arranged alphabetically by both primary plaintiff's and primary defendant's names. In addition to the parties' names and the relevant topics and key numbers, each entry includes an abbreviation for the deciding court and a citation to the case.

The Table of Cases volumes are located near the end of the digest set. They are updated through the use of pocket parts and supplements, and a list of cases by parties' names is included in the front of each advance sheet of the West reporters.

IV. Digest Coverage

The researcher must consider digest coverage when choosing in which digest to conduct research so that he will identify the digest that will send him to the cases he needs. The coverage of a digest is usually based on geography, court or court system, or subject matter.

Most digests are updated by pocket parts. In addition, some digests, like the *West's Federal Practice Digest* series, are updated by the publication of new editions in the series. Each edition covers a set period of years. The newest edition is updated by pocket parts.

A. Geography

Some digests include references to cases decided by the courts within a particular state or region. These digests are best for researching most state law issues. Choose the digest that will include citations to cases decided by courts interpreting the law applicable to the research issue. These cases will most directly assist you in identifying the law and understanding how it has been interpreted within the relevant jurisdiction.

For example, the *Louisiana Digest 2d* includes annotations to all cases reported by federal and state courts sitting in Louisiana, as well as to U.S. Fifth Circuit Court of Appeals and U.S. Supreme Court decisions originating from cases first brought in Louisiana.[4] In contrast, a digest with regional coverage, the *South Eastern Digest 2d*, includes

---

4. A state digest is available for each state except Delaware, Nevada, and Utah.

annotations to all state court decisions reported by courts in Georgia, North Carolina, South Carolina, Virginia, and West Virginia.[5]

B. Court System or Court

Some digests only include references to cases decided by the courts within a particular court system. For example, on issues of federal law, begin with a digest that specifically includes citations to cases from the federal court system, the *West's Federal Practice Digest* series. Once you identify topics and key numbers, you can focus on cases decided by the courts within your circuit if you identify a long list of cases. This series includes five sets of digests covering cases decided over different periods of time. The *West's Federal Practice Digest 4th* covers cases decided by federal courts from 1987 to date. On most issues, researchers will use this most current digest to research federal court issues because its coverage spans the last thirty plus years.

The *West's Federal Practice Digest 3d* covers cases decided by federal courts from 1975 through 1987. The *West's Federal Practice Digest 2d* covers cases decided by federal courts from 1961 through 1975. The *Modern Federal Practice Digest* covers cases decided by federal courts from 1940 through 1960. The *Federal Digest* covers cases decided by federal courts through 1939. You will probably only turn to these earlier editions of the digest when you are conducting historical research or when you are focusing on an issue that has not been litigated often.

An example of a digest that includes annotations to cases decided by a particular court is the *United States Supreme Court Digest*. This digest includes annotations to cases decided by the Unites States Supreme Court. This type of digest is helpful in those circumstances when the researcher's focus is limited to the rulings of a particular court, which will probably not be often for most researchers. Most researchers in-

---

5. Regional digests are available for cases reported in the *Atlantic Reporter*, the *North Western Reporter*, the *Pacific Reporter*, and the *South Eastern Reporter*.

terested in finding citations to Supreme Court decisions will also be interested in decisions by other federal courts, and the *West's Federal Practice Digest 4th* noted above includes citations to all of these decisions.

C. Subject Matter

Digests are also published that include references to cases decided on particular topics. Examples of these digests include *West's Bankruptcy Digest* and *West's Military Justice Digest.* Additionally, other specialized reporters such as *American Maritime Cases* and *Environment Reporter Cases* publish indices or digests periodically or as an index to the volume in which the cases are reported. The latter two digests are not West publications.

These subject matter digests are especially helpful for researching in a discrete area of law in which the number of cases decided is limited. When courts face issues that are not frequently litigated, they are usually interested not only in cases that are mandatory authority, but also in persuasive cases that provide guidance on the law and how to apply it. These digests are also helpful to the researcher who is interested in trends across jurisdictions on particular legal issues.

D. All Inclusive

The *American Digest System* refers to West's comprehensive digesting of all cases decided in the United States that are reported in the West National Reporter System. Included within this system are the *Century Digest*, which includes cases decided between 1658 and 1896, and the *Decennial Digests*, from the first edition to the eleventh, which include decisions from the subsequent ten-year periods of time. From 1976 through 1996, the *Decennial Digest* was published in two parts, one for each five-year period of the decade. The *Eleventh Decennial Digest* was published in three parts, one for 1996–2001, one for 2001–2004, and one for 2004–2007.

The *Decennial Digests* use the same topics and key numbers as the other West digests, and cases are arranged within key numbers by jurisdiction and date. Because volumes cover specific time periods, researchers must consult multiple volumes of the digest to research a period of time longer than three, five, or ten years, depending on the coverage of that particular edition. Between publications, the *General Digest* is published to update the *Decennial Digest*.

Because of their comprehensive coverage of jurisdictions and the way they are updated, these digests are not the best place to start most research projects. These digests would be helpful to the researcher who is surveying American law for a limited period of time or is trying to identify trends in American law over a limited time period. Additionally, the researcher who is looking for persuasive authority from multiple jurisdictions on an issue that has not been litigated in his jurisdiction may find this digest helpful. Otherwise, the researcher should choose to research in a more limited-coverage digest.

V. Researching Online

Cases are reported online on both free and fee-based websites. See Chapter 5, Section II.B, for a discussion of some free websites where cases are reported. This part focuses on researching cases online on the two main fee-based services, Westlaw and LexisNexis.

A. General Case Research

Similar to selecting an index or digest in which to conduct research, you need to select a *database* or *source* in which to conduct case research on Westlaw and LexisNexis. Databases are used by Westlaw and sources are used by LexisNexis to collect cases from specific jurisdictions. They sometimes combine federal and state cases from geographic areas.

Once you select a database or source, you will input a query based on your search terms that will identify relevant cases. Your query might use terms and connectors or natural language.[6] Additionally, both services allow you to search all parts of the case, including material added by publishers and concurring and dissenting opinions, or to restrict your search to only certain parts of the case, called fields or segments.

Once the search is run, you will be given a list of cases retrieved with the relevant text showing the search terms. You can choose to see the full text of the cases online or see a list of the cases with citations. You will also have easy access to updating cases retrieved, and the cases retrieved will include links to most of the sources cited within those cases.

B. Online Topic Searching

1. Westlaw Search by Topic

Westlaw allows you to restrict your search by broad topic area or by more specific digest topic and headnote. To search for cases in a database that focuses on a broad topic area, click on *Topical Practice Areas* from the Westlaw Directory. Identify the appropriate topic area for your search, then select a database that includes cases from the jurisdiction in which you are searching. For example, you might select the practice area *Products Liability*. You could then choose to search in *state cases*, and narrow your search from there by choosing Louisiana cases from the state databases list. You are ready to run a search using terms and connectors or natural language in a database that will only search Louisiana cases concerning issues of products liability. Note that the Topical Practice Areas feature allows you to search legal sources other than cases, as well.

Westlaw also allows you to search by more specific topic, using the West digest system online. From the main screen of Westlaw, you may select the *Key Numbers* tab. From this screen, you may select your jurisdiction and enter search terms to search the digest for relevant topics and key numbers, similar to searching the Descriptive-Word Index in print. This search will identify a list of topics and key numbers under which your search terms are found. From this list, choose the entries

---

6. Use of these queries is discussed more fully in Chapter 10.

that seem most relevant, then click search. You will get a listing of headnotes, just as you would get if you were looking in the print version of the digest under those topics and key numbers. Note that online the topic is represented as a number, rather than a word or phrase (*e.g.*, the topic Products Liability is assigned 313), so a topic key number online consists of two numbers separated by a "k" (*e.g.*, 313k147 represents the topic Products Liability and the key number Proximate Cause). Each headnote is assigned a topic and key number, as in print, and will include the point of law discussed, the case citation, and a link to the case.

Alternatively, from the Key Numbers screen you may click to view a listing of all West digest topics and key numbers. Once you click to this screen, you may either enter the topic number and key number separated by a *k* or you may check those topics and key numbers in which you wish to search. Then, type in your search terms and run your search. Your search will yield a list of headnotes similar to the description above.

Another possibility is to select *KeySearch* at the Key Numbers screen, which will identify thirty broad topics and many subtopics to which you can direct your search. Once you choose your topics and subtopics, you will be prompted to choose your jurisdiction and enter your search terms. You will retrieve a list of cases with citation information and links to the cases, as well as the part of the case in which your search terms are found.

Field searching on Westlaw allows you to further customize your search using some of the features of the West digest system. Field searching refers to selecting the *fields* or parts of the case in which you want the research system to search. After you choose to run a search on Westlaw in a particular database, you will have the option of using terms and connectors or natural language. You will also have the option of restricting the dates of cases in your results. Following dates you will see the field search option, which has a pull-down menu. To restrict your search to some of the features of the digest, you may choose to search the following fields: *words and phrases*, *topics*, *headnotes*, or *digest*. You may also select the shortcut to find a case by party name if you have that information available about a particular case or you may search the *title* field for a party's name.

2. LexisNexis Search by Topic

LexisNexis allows you to search a source that collects documents relevant to a broad topic area or to search by more specific topics and headnotes, similar to the Westlaw system just described. To search for cases in a source that focuses on a broad topic area, click on *Area of Law—By Topic* on the main screen of the LexisNexis research system. Identify the appropriate topic for your search, then select a source that includes cases from the jurisdiction in which you are searching.

For example, you might select the practice area *Products Liability & Toxic Torts*. Choose the *By State* link under *Find Cases*, and select the link for *LA Product Liability Cases*. Enter a terms and connectors or a natural language search and retrieve cases decided by Louisiana courts that are responsive to your search that involve product liability issues. As on Westlaw, this type of topical search can also be run to locate documents in addition to cases.

In addition, LexisNexis has developed its own system of topics and headnotes, which allows you to focus research on topics and restrict research to headnotes. Note that these topics and headnotes do not correspond directly to the topics and headnotes in West publications. To run this type of search, select the *by Topic or Headnote* tab found on the top of the main screen. You will then have the option of selecting *Find Legal Topic* or *Explore Legal Topics*. The first option prompts you to enter a description of your legal issue, after which the system will select topics that are relevant to your issue. You will then review the options and select the most relevant, after which you will be given a search screen. The second option allows you to browse topics on your own and select those that are most relevant. Once you have chosen topics, you will be given a search screen.

At the search screen, you may select the sources to search and the jurisdiction, and run a terms and connectors or natural language search. You also have a second option. You may choose a jurisdiction and run a search to retrieve all headnotes classified to the topic or cases that discuss the topic. With both of these options you may restrict your search by date.

Chapter 7

Researching Administrative Law and Other Executive Documents

This chapter discusses administrative law and other documents originating in the executive branch of government. The executive branch of government not only includes the chief political officer of a political subdivision, such as the governor of a state or the president of the United States, but also includes other elected and appointed officials and administrative agencies or departments. The law and other documents that emerge from the executive branch include administrative rules or regulations, administrative decisions, municipal charters and ordinances, executive orders and proclamations, and attorney general opinions.

This chapter describes the types of law and other documents that are issued by the executive branch of government and provides the information necessary to research these sources.

Before you begin, you should recognize a few things about researching the law and documents that emerge from the executive branch: (1) publication of these documents lacks uniformity from state to federal government, from state to state government, and even from agency to agency within the same government; (2) investigative skills will serve you well because to be effective you will often need to consult multiple sources, sometimes including executive branch personnel; and (3) updating your research is critical because most rules, regulations, and other executive documents are deemed effective upon publication in the state or federal register, which is a frequently published compilation of executive documents.

I. Overview of the Administrative Agency System

A. Administrative Agencies

Most people are familiar with the functions of administrative agencies, although many people do not realize that these agencies are part of the executive branch of government. Federal and state agencies regulate banking, insurance, health and hospitals, public safety, and environmental quality, just to name some examples.

Administrative agencies are created by the legislative branch of government to administer certain laws passed by the legislature. The federal government has a network of administrative agencies, as do each of the fifty states. Louisiana defines the term *agency* to include:

> each state board, commission, department, agency, officer, or other entity which makes rules, regulations, or policy, or formulates, or issues decisions or orders pursuant to, or as directed by, or in implementation of the constitution or laws of the United States or the constitution and statutes of Louisiana.[1]

This definition includes governmental entities that are not part of the legislative or judicial branches of government. It generally describes the term *agency* as it is used in the federal government and in other state governments, as well.

Agencies perform functions within the bounds of an *administrative procedure act* and an *enabling act*. The Louisiana Administrative Procedure Act[2] dictates the procedures necessary for Louisiana agencies to create rules, contains information about the publication and

---

1. La. Rev. Stat. Ann. §49:951(2) (Supp. 2013). Louisiana's definition of agency excludes "the legislature or any branch, committee, or officer thereof, any political subdivision, as defined in Article VI, Section 44 of the Louisiana Constitution, and any board, commission, department, agency, officer, or other entity thereof, and the courts."

2. La. Rev. Stat. Ann. §§49:950–:972 (2003 & Supp. 2013).

distribution of these rules, and establishes the procedural rules for adjudicating violations of administrative law. Similar to the Louisiana act, the federal Administrative Procedure Act[3] mandates the various procedures to be used by federal governmental agencies.

Each agency's authority is governed by that agency's enabling act or enabling legislation. The enabling act is the legislation or constitutional provision from which the agency draws its power to act. It defines the purposes and the scope of the agency.

Typically, agencies are created to administer and oversee government programs and to monitor and regulate certain industries. To do so, agencies promulgate *rules* or *regulations*[4] that specifically identify how the laws are to be administered. Agencies also apply those rules or regulations to covered individuals and entities in administrative hearings.

B. Agency Rules

Administrative rules and regulations are considered primary authority, but they are subordinate to the statutes and constitutional provisions from which the agencies get their authority. Rules and regulations passed by administrative agencies are typically more specific than legislative statutes, and they address the technical details of the law in a particular field. Before the adoption or amendment of any rule, the agency will often study the topic and gather expert opinions on the topic. Also, procedural rules usually require the agency to allow the public to respond to any proposed rules or changes in rules before those rules are adopted or amended.

C. Agency Hearings

Agencies also conduct administrative hearings. When a dispute arises over an agency's application of a rule or regulation, the person

---

3. 5 U.S.C.A. §§ 551 *et seq.* (West 2007 & Supp. 2012).

4. The terms *rules* and *regulations* are both used to refer to rules coming from administrative agencies. The term *rule* is used in Louisiana, while the term *regulation* is most often used in the federal system.

Louisiana Lagniappe 7-1.

ALJ Rulings

Louisiana is the first and may be the only state in which an agency is unable to appeal an adverse ruling made by an ALJ from a central panel, like the Division of Administrative Law. The significance of this limitation is that the central panel ALJ, an agency outsider who may not have any expertise on the subject being regulated, is able to have the final say in the particular case on interpreting the agency's regulations. *See* April Rolen-Ogden, Student Author, *When Administrative Law Judges Rule the World: Wooley v. State Farm–Does a Denial of Agency-Initiated Judicial Review of ALJ Final Orders Violate the Constitutional Doctrine of Separation of Powers?*, 66 La. L. Rev. 885 (2006), and sources cited therein.

---

or entity against whom the rule is being applied may request a hearing from the agency. An administrative law judge (ALJ) will hear the dispute and render a decision as to the propriety of the action taken.

In Louisiana, the hearing will be held either by an ALJ from within the agency or by an ALJ from the *Division of Administrative Law*. The Division of Administrative Law is an independent state agency charged with holding administrative law hearings of disputes originating in many state agencies.[5] Disputes over the application of federal regulations are usually handled by ALJs from the federal agencies involved or by federal agencies designated to hear certain types of disputes, such as the National Labor Relations Board.

If a person or entity is not satisfied with the decision rendered by the ALJ, usually the person or entity can seek review of the decision in the judicial system. See Louisiana Lagniappe 7-1.

---

5. The Division of Administrative Law is governed by La. Rev. Stat. Ann. §§ 49:991–:999.1 (Supp. 2013).

D. Example of an Agency

An example of a state agency is the Louisiana Board of Elementary and Secondary Education (BESE), which was created by a provision in the Louisiana Constitution of 1974 to serve as a body that would administer elementary and secondary education in the state. On its website, BESE identifies its main duties:

- Enacting policies and adopting regulations governing the state-wide operations of public and nonpublic elementary and secondary schools, including special schools and entities in Special School District #1;
- Exercising administrative oversight over functions of the state's three special schools (blind, deaf, physically handicapped), and Special School Districts #1 and #2, including personnel, budget, and program operations;
- Administering and serving as the fiscal agent and as program control agent for the Education Quality Trust Fund 8(g) programs;
- Conducting administrative hearings and serving as the "court of last resort" prior to judicial proceedings in cases/controversies deriving from Board actions;
- Exercising budgetary and fiscal control over the educational programs and services at the elementary and secondary (state and federal funds);
- Preparing the MFP [Minimum Foundation Program] and presenting it to the Legislature for approval and distributing funds to local school systems.[6]

Note the key agency functions of enacting policies and rules, administering programs, and conducting hearings.

---

6. State of Louisiana, Department of Education, Board of Elementary and Secondary Education, http://doe.louisiana.gov/bese/history.html.

II. Louisiana Administrative Rules

The majority of Louisiana's administrative rules can be found in two publications, the *Louisiana Administrative Code* (LAC) and the *Louisiana Register*, both of which are published by the Louisiana Office of the State Register, in print and online. The LAC is a codified version of Louisiana's administrative rules that is organized by general subject matter into numbered titles. Individual titles are published in print every two years, reflecting any amendments, deletions, or other changes that have occurred during the interim. A table of contents precedes the rules in each title. An *authority note* following each rule provides a citation to the enabling act or the legislative or constitutional authority for the rule, and an *historical note* identifies which agency promulgated the rule and when. The LAC does not have a comprehensive index in print, but a subject index can be found on the Office of the State Register's website at www.doa.louisiana.gov/osr/osr.htm, under the *Louisiana Administrative Code* link on the left-hand side of the website.

Titles in the LAC are numbered between one and seventy-six, although only thirty-four of the numbers in that series are currently being used. Numbers that have been skipped and are not currently being used allow for the addition of new titles within the series. Some examples of the subject areas of titles include *Education, Environmental Quality, Louisiana Gaming*, and *Natural Resources*. A citation or reference to a rule in the LAC includes the title number, which is an Arabic number, as well as the part, a Roman numeral, and the section, another Arabic number. Although the rules also include subparts, chapters, and subchapters before the section number, the numbering is consecutive across these divisions so they need not be identified when referencing a rule.

An example rule is shown in Figure 7-1. This rule is found in Title 43, Natural Resources, Part I, Subpart 1, Chapter 7, Subchapter B, Section 717. A citation to this section would be written as follows: La. Admin. Code tit. 43, § I.717 (2008) (according to the *ALWD Citation Manual* and *The Bluebook*), or LAC 43:I.717 (2008) (sometimes used in practice in Louisiana).

Figure 7-1. Excerpt from LAC

§ 717. **Guidelines for Uses that Result in the Alteration of Waters Draining into Coastal Waters**

A. Upland and upstream water management programs which affect coastal waters and wetlands shall be designed and constructed to preserve or enhance existing water quality, volume, and rate of flow to the maximum extent practicable.

B. Runoff from developed areas shall to the maximum extent practicable be managed to simulate natural water patterns, quantity, quality, and rate of flow.

C. Runoff and erosion from agricultural lands shall be minimized through the best practical techniques.

AUTHORITY NOTE: Promulgated in accordance with R.S. 49:214.27.

HISTORICAL NOTE: Promulgated by the Department of Natural Resources, Office of the Secretary, LR 6:493 (August 1980).

The *Louisiana Register* is a monthly publication of revised or newly approved agency rules and notices of intent for proposed changes to rules. Most agency rules become effective upon publication in the *Louisiana Register*, even though it may be some time before they are incorporated into and published in the LAC. The *Louisiana Register* also publishes emergency rules,[7] executive orders,[8] and potpourri.[9] A table of contents identifies each of these categories and identifies the agencies that have published material under each category during that month. Additionally, each issue includes a cumulative index that contains references to the current issue and all of the previous monthly issues of the *Louisiana Register* for that calendar year.

---

7. An emergency rule is a temporary adaptation of a rule because of an emergency situation.

8. An executive order is an order issued by the governor, which is discussed later in this chapter.

9. The potpourri section is a miscellaneous section containing a variety of public notices by agencies, such as notices of licensing exams to be given and notices of agency plans to take future action.

Like the LAC, the *Louisiana Register* is available online on the Office of the State Register's website at www.doa.louisiana.gov/osr/osr.htm, under the *Louisiana Register* link on the left-hand side of the website. Although the print version of the LAC is the official version, the online version on the government website is more frequently updated from the *Louisiana Register* than are other versions. Changes reported in the *Louisiana Register* usually appear in the government's online version of the LAC within a few weeks of the *Louisiana Register*'s publication.

Despite the fact that most of Louisiana's administrative laws are found within the LAC and the *Louisiana Register*, some state agencies do not publish their rules in either publication. For example, the Department of Civil Service's rules are not published in any title of the LAC but can be found on its website, www.civilservice.la.gov. For this reason and because many agency websites include links to relevant sections of the LAC, an agency's website is a good place to begin research when you know which agency administers the area of law you are researching. Websites also often include agency forms and information about agency policies and procedures. An alphabetical listing of Louisiana agencies with links to corresponding websites can be found at http://louisiana.gov/Government/Agency_Index.

III. Researching Louisiana Administrative Rules

Where you begin your research in administrative law depends on what information you already know about the area of law that governs your legal issue. This part explains how to begin research in an unfamiliar area of law, with limited knowledge, and with a citation to a rule. Regardless of how you begin, administrative rule research must be updated, which is covered at the end of this part.

A. Researching an Unfamiliar Area of Law

If you are unfamiliar with the area of law, but you know or suspect that the area of law is governed by administrative rules, consider beginning your research in a secondary authority, like a practice guide or a deskbook on the subject. These types of authorities are discussed in Chapter 9. A practice guide written for lawyers who practice in a particular area of law will identify the primary sources of law that govern the field, including administrative rules.

B. Researching with Limited Knowledge of an Area of Law

If you have some knowledge about the area of law, you might still benefit from beginning research in a secondary authority, like a deskbook or practice guide on the subject. As discussed below, you may also decide to begin by using your search terms and scanning the list of state agencies, the LAC Subject Index, and the list of titles to the LAC, all of which are available online at the websites identified earlier. Research on a fee-based online service can also be an effective way to research administrative law.

1. State Agency List

If you choose to begin with the list of state agencies, you should scan the list for agencies that seem relevant to your issue. After identifying agencies that seem relevant, go to the agency websites to determine if the agencies handle and regulate issues like the one you are researching. To do this, review the enabling statute for the agency to determine the purpose of the agency and the scope of its authority. The website will probably have a direct link to the enabling statute. The enabling statute will also be referenced in the authority note that follows agency rules, as is seen in Figure 7-1.

Agency websites also often provide links to relevant rules and other related resources. If you are still not sure if the agency handles and regulates the issue you are researching, search for cases that have interpreted the enabling statute to determine the agency's relevancy to the issue you are researching. Researching statutes is discussed in Chapter 3, and researching cases is discussed in Chapters 5 and 6.

Finally, a phone call to the agency to ask agency personnel about the agency's rules and procedures and how they have been interpreted can also prove beneficial. Contact information is available on agency websites. Although you would not want to rely solely on the information gleaned through a phone call, agency personnel may provide information unique to the agency that will steer you in the right direction in your research.

For example, if you were researching an environmental issue, scanning the list of Louisiana administrative agencies would lead you to the Louisiana Department of Environmental Quality. The department's website is located at www.deq.louisiana.gov/portal. You could locate the site either through the link on the state's list of agencies or by using a search engine on the Internet and typing in key words such as *Louisiana environment agency*. Once you locate the site, a menu on the left-hand side includes a link to rules and regulations. This link takes you to valuable information such as links to state rules, related federal regulations, and the enabling statute for the agency. It also includes a listing of current emergency rules, a monthly update of rule changes, and a schedule of public hearings on proposed rules. Further, the link provides some brief advice on researching environmental rules and a phone number to call for assistance.

2. LAC Subject Index and List of LAC Titles

Two other ways to begin research are by using search terms in the LAC Subject Index or in the list of titles to the LAC. Links to these documents are located on the Office of the State Register's website at www.doa.louisiana.gov/osr/osr.htm, under the *Louisiana Administrative Code* link. Using your search terms in the subject index, you will find references to potentially relevant LAC titles and parts within those titles. For most titles, you may click on the index entry to access the title, which is linked to the LAC. Otherwise, record the potentially relevant titles and parts, then locate them either online or in print. Using your search terms to scan titles of the LAC may also lead to relevant rules.

Once you locate potentially relevant titles and parts, search the tables of contents of the titles to focus on relevant rules. This task may be done either in print or online. As with statutory research, once you identify potentially relevant rules, read the rules carefully to determine their relevance to the issue you are researching and be sure to update the rules.

3. Fee-Based Online Services

Both Westlaw and LexisNexis have the LAC and the *Louisiana Register* available on their websites. These services allow searching in administrative law databases using search terms. This method can be effective if you have developed a list of search terms that are precise enough to focus on the language that is found in the rules, but that are not too broad to yield an overwhelming number of documents. For example, a search in a database of Louisiana administrative rules for the word *environment* yielded 801 documents. The search identified all rules using the word, even rules that have nothing to do with rules governing the environment. Thus, you must be careful in crafting search terms, which is discussed in more detail in Chapter 2.

C. Researching With a Citation to a Relevant Rule

If you have been given a citation to a rule or rules, or you have located citations to a rule or rules using the methods set forth above, locate the rule either online or in print in the LAC. Read the rule carefully to assess its relevance to the research issue and to determine its meaning. Skim the table of contents of the title in which the rule is found for related rules, such as rules that define terms or set out procedures for enforcement of other rules. Check any cross references provided in or following the rule. Review the historical note following the rule to determine when it was promulgated and if and when it has been amended. Frequent amendments may suggest trends in the way the law has shifted over time to predict future changes. To determine the specific changes in the rule, locate the copy of the *Louisiana Register* for the months in which the rule was amended.

Review the authority note for a citation to the enabling act for the agency. The enabling act will provide information about the purpose of the agency and the scope of its authority, which may assist in interpreting the rule and in determining if the rule is within the agency's power. Additionally, checking the annotations to the enabling act may provide information on how the rule or similar rules have been interpreted by the courts. Similarly, agency personnel and agency publications may also assist in determining how the rules have been interpreted within the agency. Unlike the codes in which legislation is found, such as the *Louisiana Civil Code Annotated* discussed in Chapter 3, the LAC is not annotated with case references.

One note about whether to begin in the print or the online version of the LAC: the version of the LAC online on the government website is updated more frequently than is the print version. Changes reported in the *Louisiana Register* usually appear in the government's online version of the LAC within a few weeks of the *Louisiana Register*'s publication; thus, you probably want to research online. Then, if you need to cite the provision to a court, cite the print version as supplemented with the *Louisiana Register*.

D. Updating Rules

As in most legal research, updating administrative rules is essential. Both the online and print versions of the LAC include the compilation date of the title or the date the title was last updated in the LAC. Titles in the LAC are recompiled or reprinted about every two years. However, rules promulgated by agencies usually become effective upon publication in the monthly *Louisiana Register*, which means that the researcher will need to determine what changes to the rules have taken place between the compilation date of the LAC title and the date of the research. (As noted earlier, the government online version of the LAC is updated more frequently than the LAC print version is published.)

To properly update, you will need to check three features of the *Louisiana Register*: the *annual administrative code update*; the *administrative code update*, which is published quarterly; and the *cumulative index*. First, check the annual administrative code update, which is published in the January issue of the *Louisiana Register*. This up-

Table 7-1. Illustration of How to Update LAC Research

Assume that the rule you are researching is found in LAC Title 33, Part V, of the Environmental Quality rules, which shows a compilation date of September 2011. Updating this title and part in December 2012 would include the following steps:

(1) Check the annual administrative code update for the year 2011 in the January 2012 issue of the *Louisiana Register* under Title 33.

(2) Check the administrative code update in the October 2012 issue of the *Louisiana Register* under Title 33.

(3) Check the cumulative index of the December 2012 issue of the *Louisiana Register* under Environmental Quality, then locate any referenced actions to determine their effect on the rule in which you are interested.

date is a chart that is organized by title number. The chart identifies any changes that have taken place in any of the titles of the LAC during the previous calendar year. Use this chart for each year since the compilation date of the title you are researching.

Second, if at least a quarter of a year has passed, check the April, July, or October issues of the *Louisiana Register* for the administrative code update; this version of the update includes a cumulative chart of changes that have taken place during the previous quarter or quarters of that calendar year. This update is usually found in Section V or VI of the *Louisiana Register* for those months.

Third, use the cumulative index for any remaining parts of a year to determine if any changes have been made. This index is organized by agency, not title, and it sends the researcher to the page number of the *Louisiana Register* on which the agency action is reported. See Table 7-1 for an example of how to update a rule in the LAC.

Although this updating may be done in print, you may find it quicker to switch from document to document electronically on the Office of the State Register's website.

IV. Other Documents from the Louisiana Executive Branch

A. Miscellaneous State Agency Documents

In addition to publishing rules, state agencies often publish other resources for the public on their websites, such as contact information for agency officials, manuals for rule compliance, records of enforcement actions, forms, public notices, and news releases. These documents can assist the lawyer in interpreting agency rules as well as in servicing clients' needs.

Additionally, state agencies hold hearings when a dispute arises as to the application of their rules. In Louisiana, most agencies send disputes to be heard by an administrative law judge in the Division of Administrative Law, while some agencies hold their own hearings. The opinions resulting from these hearings are not available online and are not easily researchable, although they may be obtained from the Division of Administrative Law or the particular agency. However, should a party choose to appeal a hearing decision in the court system, a record of the resulting litigation may be available. See Chapters 5 and 6 on researching cases.

B. Municipal Law

Municipal law includes *municipal charters*, which are to municipalities what a constitution is to a state, and *municipal ordinances*, which are similar to state administrative rules. Municipal charters and ordinances are considered primary authority governing particular cities, towns, or parishes within the state of Louisiana. All municipal charters and ordinances in Louisiana are available at www.municode.com, which has a searchable database. Links to this website are available through most municipal websites.

C. Executive Orders and Proclamations

Executive orders and proclamations from the governor have the force of law. *Executive orders* address such issues as bond allocations, the setting of salaries for executive board members, and even the ordering of flags in the state to be flown at half staff in honor of a fallen citizen. These orders may be found online at http://doa.louisiana.gov/osr/other/exord.htm. They are listed by the name of the governor and the year of the order. They are labeled with the governor's initials, the year, and the number of the order in that year, such as Executive Order BJ 13-01, indicating Governor Bobby Jindal's first executive order in 2013.

Executive proclamations include such things as the proclamation of a state of emergency after a severe weather event, the proclamation that a special election will be held, and the call for the convening of a special legislative session. These documents may be found at www.gov.state.la.us/index.cfm by selecting *Official Documents* from the *Newsroom* menu, then clicking on *View Executive Proclamations*. They are referenced by the number of the proclamation in the year, the governor's initials, and the year, such as Executive Proclamation 31 BJ 2013. See Louisiana Lagniappe 7-2 for references to some noteworthy uses of executive orders and proclamations.

Louisiana Lagniappe 7-2.
Executive Orders
Following Hurricanes Katrina and Rita in 2005, Louisiana Governor Kathleen Blanco used the executive power given to her by statute to act in emergencies to issue many executive orders. These orders did such things as suspend prescription and other legal deadlines, commandeer property for state use, suspend state license requirements for out-of-state doctors and veterinarians who came to assist in the state, order hotels to allow evacuees to remain in their rooms, and delay elections. She also used executive proclamations to declare states of emergency.

D. Attorney General Opinions

The attorney general is the lawyer for the state. In performing this role, the attorney general issues written opinions to governmental entities and officers about issues involving state law, similar to advice an attorney would give a client. While only a source of persuasive authority, Louisiana attorney general opinions can be helpful when trying to interpret state law and understand the propriety of the actions of parties under state law. Attorney general opinions are archived dating back to 1977 and are available on the Internet at www.ag.state.la.us/Opinions.aspx. You may search these opinions by search terms and by year on this site.

V. Federal Administrative Law

Federal agencies function similar to state agencies, but federal administrative law is somewhat easier to research than most state administrative law because it is usually better catalogued and indexed. For example, the *Washington Information Dictionary* contains a list of subjects and provides a description of agencies that deal with each subject. Also, the *United States Government Manual*, the official handbook of the federal government, is a comprehensive source for obtaining general information about all three branches of government, with a concentration on the executive branch. The *United States Government Manual* lists the objectives, contact information, websites, and other information for almost every agency, board, or commission in the federal government. It is available in print at all federal depository libraries. It is also available online at www.usgovernmentmanual.gov.

Another online list of agencies with links to agency websites and other resources is Louisiana State University's Federal Agencies Directory, which can be found at www.lib.lsu.edu/gov. Agency websites can be a great source for citations to agency regulations, enabling acts, policies, reports, specific contact information, and other useful information.

A. *Code of Federal Regulations*

Federal administrative rules are called *regulations*. Regulations are published in the *Code of Federal Regulations* (CFR) and in the *Federal Register*. The CFR is a codification of the regulations promulgated by federal administrative agencies, similar to the LAC. The regulations are organized by general subject area and are contained in fifty subject-specific titles, which are numbered one through fifty. The *United States Government Manual* lists all agencies whose regulations appear in the CFR along with the titles and subtitles or chapters in which the agencies' regulations appear. Additionally, on the back of every issue of the CFR is an alphabetical list of the agencies whose regulations appear in that title with their corresponding chapters for easy referencing.

The CFR is updated annually, with a different set of titles updated each quarter of the year. Titles 1–16 are updated with revisions made as of January 1; titles 17–27 are updated with revisions made as of April 1; titles 28–41 are updated with revisions made as of July 1; and titles 42–50 are updated with revisions made as of October 1. Printed and online copies of the updated titles are released usually within a couple of months of the end of the quarter date. A researcher can quickly tell if a volume of the CFR has been updated during the present year. A different color for the cover of the printed CFR titles is used each year to differentiate those that have been updated and those that have not.

The Government Printing Office publishes the CFR online at www.gpoaccess.gov/cfr/index.html. The date of the last revision precedes the text of the title. Another unofficial, but updated, version of the CFR can be found by clicking on *e-CFR* from the CFR main page. The CFR is also available on the websites of LexisNexis, Westlaw, HeinOnline, and FindLaw, although dates of coverage vary by site.

B. *Federal Register*

Prior to publication in the CFR, where regulations are placed in their proper titles by subject area, regulations are published in the *Federal Register*. The *Federal Register* is published nearly every business day with a continuous page count throughout the year. Regulations are published here as they are promulgated. The *Federal Register* is the first available source for new federal administrative regulations. Serving a purpose similar to that of the *Louisiana Register*, the *Federal Register* publishes the following: (1) presidential documents, such as executive orders; (2) rules and regulations; (3) proposed rules; and (4) notices, such as of meetings and of application deadlines. It also includes extensive background information underlying regulation changes, which is not published in the CFR. This information can serve as a good tool in understanding regulations and the policies behind them.

A table of contents preceding each issue of the *Federal Register* is organized by agency and by classification of the document. An attorney who needs to keep up with regulatory changes involving a particular industry will skim the relevant agency headings in the table of contents of each *Federal Register* as it is published to see if anything has been issued affecting his clients. The best access to the *Federal Register* is provided online by the G.P.O., at www.fdsys.gov, where it is updated every day by 6:00 a.m. It is browsable and searchable. The Office of the Federal Register and the G.P.O. also maintain "Federal Register 2.0," a daily web newspaper-formatted presentation of the information contained in each daily *Federal Register* issue.[10] You may also view the contents of the *Federal Register* on the websites of LexisNexis, Westlaw, HeinOnline, and FindLaw.

Additionally, the CFR and the *Federal Register* are available in print in all federal depository libraries and in many law libraries.

VI. Researching Federal Administrative Law

As is the case with researching Louisiana administrative law, where you begin your research depends on what information you already know about the area of law that governs your legal issue. Consult the previous section in this chapter on researching Louisiana administrative law for some tips on where to begin. This section will supplement that section by highlighting tools specific to federal regulation research.

---

10. *See* www.federalregister.gov.

A. Identify the Relevant Agency

When possible, identify the agency that has jurisdiction over your issue and consult the agency's website and personnel to understand how the agency is structured and what the agency's goals are. As is mentioned above, the *United States Government Manual* lists all agencies whose regulations appear in the CFR along with where the agencies' regulations appear. Additionally, on the back of every issue of the CFR is an alphabetical list of the agencies that appear in that title with their corresponding chapters for easy referencing. Thus, these sources are good places to begin your research when you know which agency governs your issue.

B. Search for Relevant Regulations in the CFR

You may research regulations in the CFR either in print or online. To research a regulation in the CFR in print, use search terms in the CFR Index and Finding Aids, which is a subject index that is a part of the CFR publication. This index may provide citations to regulations on your research issue.

To research regulations online, you may use search terms to search the online versions of the CFR on the websites mentioned in Part V above. The version of the CFR on the government site is only updated as frequently as the printed text, but it is considered the official version. The versions on Westlaw and LexisNexis and the e-CFR are updated more frequently, but they are not considered official versions.

C. Search for References to Regulations Using an Annotated Code

Annotated publications of the United States Code, especially the *United States Code Service*, will provide cross references to relevant federal regulations. Thus, you may begin your search using search terms in the index to an annotated code to find relevant statutes that will cross reference regulations or you may use a citation you already have for a statute to do the same.

D. Locate Cases Interpreting Federal Regulations

As is true when researching statutes, locating judicial interpretations of regulations can be valuable to the researcher. Although the CFR is not annotated, you may find references to cases in which regulations have been interpreted in the annotations to related federal statutes. Moreover, you can use *Shepard's* on LexisNexis or KeyCite on Westlaw to find citations to cases and other secondary sources in which the regulation has been cited. Using Shepard's Citators and KeyCite is discussed in Chapter 8.

E. Updating Federal Regulations

Federal administrative regulations change frequently, so it is important to update your research to ensure that you have found regulations that are still in force. The simplest way to do this is to use Lexis-Nexis or Westlaw or e-CFR, all of which update the CFR frequently based on changes published in the *Federal Register*. Each of these services will indicate how up to date the material is.

To verify a federal regulation in print, first locate the *List of CFR Sections Affected* (LSA), which is usually located following the last edition of the CFR. The LSA lists all of the sections of the CFR that have been affected by changes made to the regulations since the CFR was published. To determine if any changes have been made, look for the section you are researching in the LSA. If it is not listed in the LSA, then the regulation was not changed during the period covered by that issue of the LSA. If the regulation is listed, there will be a reference to a page in the *Federal Register* where the change is identified.

Second, go to the last issue of the *Federal Register* in each month since the LSA date. Turn to a section called *CFR Parts Affected During* [*the current month*]. Be sure to check the last issue of each month from the most recent LSA to the current date. Finally, check the most recent issue of the *Federal Register* in the current month for updates. Both the LSA and the CFR Parts Affected During [the current month] are available in print as well as online at www.gpoaccess.gov/lsa/curlist.html.

The free, online issues of *Federal Register* at the FDsys website are more current than the print version.

VII. Other Documents from the Federal Executive Branch

A. Decisions of Federal Agencies

Similar to Louisiana agencies, federal agencies hold hearings to resolve disputes arising from the agency's regulations. Some of these decisions are published in reporters specific to each agency, and some are published on agency websites. A list of some federal administrative publications can be found in Appendix 8 to the *ALWD Citation Manual*. A comprehensive listing of agencies with links to opinions can be found at www.washlaw.edu/doclaw/executive5m.html. Further, Westlaw and LexisNexis have topical databases that include the decisions of some agencies.

B. Executive Orders and Proclamations

Executive orders and proclamations are published in the *Federal Register* and are available both in print and online. They are available online on several of the federal government websites mentioned previously in this chapter, most of which allow searching. Additionally, these documents are easily located using web browsers like Google and Yahoo!, which link to government and other websites.

Chapter 8

Updating

Updating means checking sources to find out if acts subsequent to their publication have changed their viability or their contents. Updating is also often referred to as *Shepardizing* or *KeyCiting*, named for the two primary updating sources.

A lawyer has an ethical obligation to provide *competent representation* to a client, which includes acting with "the legal knowledge, skill, thoroughness and preparation reasonably necessary for the representation."[1] A lawyer is also required to exercise candor toward a tribunal, which includes obligations to accurately state the law to the court and to correct any false statements of law previously made by the lawyer to the tribunal.[2] Complying with these obligations includes the duty to properly research the governing law and ensure that the law on which an argument is based is good law. See Louisiana Lagniappe 8-1.

In addition to an ethical obligation, one of the most embarrassing things that can happen to an attorney or someone working with an attorney is reliance on a source that is no longer good or has been modified in some way. This embarrassment need not happen because the tools available for updating are accurate, available, and easy to use.

Each chapter in this book addresses the issue of updating the particular sources being discussed in the chapter. This chapter provides an overview of updating to augment those sections.

---

1. La. Rules Prof. Conduct 1.1(a).
2. *Id.* at 3.3(a).

I. The Benefits of Updating

The benefits of updating are two-fold: (1) to ensure that sources on which you rely are still good law; and (2) to gather citations to additional sources relevant to the legal issue and relevant to the source being updated.

> ### Louisiana Lagniappe 8-1.
>
> **Updating Briefs and Arguments**
>
> The Louisiana Supreme Court specifically recognizes a lawyer's continuing obligations to the court in Supreme Court rule VII, which provides a procedure for lawyers to follow to supplement their briefs and arguments should they become aware of authorities that affect arguments made to the court. Rule VII, section 11.2, provides: "If pertinent and significant authorities come to a party's attention after all original and reply briefs have been filed—or after oral argument but before decision—a party may promptly advise the clerk by letter, with a copy to all other parties, setting forth the citations."

Law changes over time to meet the needs of society and to adapt to new circumstances. Constitutions, statutes, rules, and regulations are amended or repealed or deemed unconstitutional. Court decisions are reversed or overruled. Even when court decisions are not overruled, they may be questioned and criticized by other courts, which may weaken their viability for the future. You need to be aware of the viability and the strength of your sources so that you can accurately predict whether the law will be applied to the issue you are researching and how it will be applied.

Updating also serves as a research tool to locate additional sources on the issue being researched. Updating will provide you with citations to all sources that have cited the source you are checking. This list may include both primary and secondary sources.

II. Where to Update

Updating should be done in two places. First, check the book or website in which you are researching to ensure you have its most current material. Second, use a *citator*. A citator collects and lists all sources that have cited to the source you are updating. The *cited source* is the source you are updating. The *citing source* is the source that has cited to the source you are updating.

A. Using the Source in Which You are Researching

When researching in a print source, check for a pocket part or supplement to the print source and ensure that you are working in the current volume of the source. Pocket parts are located in the pocket of the front or back cover of the book; supplements should be located just behind the book in which you are researching or at the end of the set of books in which you are researching. Pocket parts and supplements will identify when they were published and what volumes of books they are meant to supplement. This information often appears on their front covers.

Also, be sure you have the most recent volume of that source. If not updated by pocket parts or supplements, or sometimes in addition to pocket parts and supplements, print sources may be updated by the publication of a new edition. Often, earlier editions will be removed from library shelves. To ensure that you are working in the current edition of the source, check the date of any pocket part or supplement to determine if it is current. If the pocket part of the source in which you are researching seems to be out of date, you may not be researching in the current edition of the source. For a source not updated by pocket parts, check the library catalog to determine if any later editions of the source are available.

When researching online, check the currentness of the source on the website. For example, if you are researching a statute online, the site may indicate that the information is current through the end of a particular legislative session or through a particular date.

B. Using a Citator

Louisiana Lagniappe 8-2.

From Print to Online Updating

For years, *Shepard's Citations* in print was the dominant source for updating. As electronic researching developed, both Lexis-Nexis and Westlaw carried Shepard's online. To ensure a market for the print product, the online product and the print product were updated at the same time so that neither was more current than the other. Eventually, Lexis-Nexis acquired exclusive rights to Shepard's, and Westlaw developed KeyCite to compete with Shepard's online. Today, the online products are more current than are the print products.

Once you have updated using the sources in which you are researching, you should turn to citators to complete the updating process. Citators are available both in print and online. The online citators are more up to date than the print products, and they should be used whenever possible. See Louisiana Lagniappe 8-2, and Part IV of this chapter. Even the literature on Shepard's in print produced by its owner recommends the online product over the print product. For this reason, this chapter will focus on electronic citators.

The most respected and complete citators available online are Shepard's, available on LexisNexis, and KeyCite, available on Westlaw.[3] Both online citators share some common characteristics.

1. Updating on Both Services Is Simple and User-Friendly

Once you enter your password, you are given an option on each service to enter a citation on an initial screen and click to KeyCite or

---

3. Other online citators that are not as complete or as well respected include "V.Cite" on VersusLaw, "How cited" on Google Scholar, "CASEcheck" on Casemaker, "Authority Check" on Fastcase, "BCite" on Bloomberg Law, and "GlobalCite" on Loislaw.

Shepardize from that screen. You need not select a database for research. You also have the option of choosing to KeyCite or Shepardize at any time during your research, either by typing in a citation or clicking on a document you are viewing that can be updated on these services. Additionally, both services provide links to explanations about how to use their updating systems and how to interpret the results. Table 8-1 provides an outline for using a citator.

Table 8-1. Outline for Using a Citator

1. Access the desired citator list.
2. Analyze the analytical symbols provided by the citator.
3. Consider limiting the list of citing references by jurisdiction, headnote, date, or other function.
4. Prioritize and read the citing sources.
   a. To validate, analyze the impact, if any, these sources have on the cited source.
   b. To expand research, decide whether the citing sources provide clearer explanations of the law, analyze facts that are closer to your client's, or otherwise impact your issue in significant ways.

2. Two Types of Citing Lists with Links to Citing Sources Allow Easy Review of Results

While you are viewing the results of updating on these services, most citations in the results have links you may click to view the sources retrieved. This feature makes checking the citing sources convenient.

Each service provides two lists of citing sources, one directed to the researcher who is simply validating a source to ensure that it is still good law, and a second directed to the researcher who is still researching to find additional authorities on a point of law. The first list is a shorter list that includes the history of the source you are checking as well as negative citing references. On Westlaw this list is labeled *KeyCite Full History*; on LexisNexis this list is labeled *KWIC* and *Shepard's for Validation*. The second list is a list of citing sources that is helpful for continuing research because it includes citations to additional sources on the point of law you are researching. On Westlaw this list is labeled *KeyCite Citing References*; on LexisNexis it is labeled *Full* and *Shepard's for Research*.

3. Signals Assist in Interpreting Results

Each service provides a system of signals or symbols to assist you in interpreting the results of updating.

a. Shepard's

Shepard's on LexisNexis provides a result summary to allow you to immediately know the results of your search, which is accompanied by a signal indicating the type of treatment the source has received. For example, a red octagon signals strong negative treatment by subsequent citing sources, while a green diamond indicates positive treatment. Holding your cursor on any of the signals will reveal the meaning of the signal. Alternatively, you may click on the word *legend* on the bottom of the screen to see the legend for all of the signals used by Shepard's.

You may also use the *All Neg*, *All Pos*, and *FOCUS* features to tailor your results. *All Neg* will reveal only citing sources that have negatively treated the cited case; *All Pos* will reveal positive citing sources. *FOCUS* allows you to restrict the results you view by jurisdiction, headnote, date, type of treatment, type of citing document, and terms you enter.

b. KeyCite

KeyCite on Westlaw uses *status flags* and *depth of treatment* stars to signal the type of treatment given to the cited source by the citing sources. For example, a red flag indicates that the source is no longer good law, a yellow flag indicates some negative history, and a green C indicates the existence of citing references that are not negative. As with Shepard's online, holding the cursor on any of these symbols reveals its meaning. Depth of treatment stars are used as signals as well, with four stars indicating that the cited source was examined in the citing source, down through one star indicating that the cited source was only briefly mentioned. When using KeyCite to update a case, the result also identifies the headnotes from the cited case that correspond to the points discussed in the citing source.

Much like the feature on LexisNexis Shepard's that allows you to tailor the results of your updating result, clicking on *Limit KeyCite Display* on Westlaw allows you options to limit your results by jurisdiction, headnote, date, depth of treatment, document type, and terms you enter.

4. A Wide Variety of Sources May Be Updated

Both services provide updating of a wide variety of sources. Sources that can be updated on both services include federal and state cases and statutes; federal and state constitutions; federal and some states' administrative rules or regulations, including Louisiana rules; federal and state court rules; some federal administrative decisions; patents; *American Law Reports* (ALR); and some law review articles. Each service varies from the other on the exact list of sources that may be updated.

5. A Wide Variety of Potential Sources Are Searched

Both services search a wide variety of potential citing sources, including both primary and secondary sources, legislative documents, and court documents.

III. Limitations on Results of Updating with Citators

Using citators to update research is a critical step in conducting thorough research. However, citators have their limitations. Citators only identify cases and other citing sources that actually cite to the case or other cited source being updated. They do *not* indicate that the rule or principle in the cited source on which you are relying was changed, such as overruled, *unless* the overruling case mentions the cited source.

For example, you might rely on a case called *Smith v. Jones* as authority for use of a particular test by the court in your jurisdiction. A court in a case decided subsequent to *Smith v. Jones* might overrule the use of that test in the jurisdiction in favor of another test, but the court in the second case might fail to cite *Smith v. Jones* in its opinion. Shepardizing or KeyCiting *Smith v. Jones* will not reveal the overruling case if the second court did not cite to *Smith v. Jones*. Your research needs to be thorough enough that you would have found authorities for your jurisdiction on the issue, rather than just relying on one of the updating services to tell you that you have good law based on one source.

An additional limitation on the use of citators is that the citators categorize the treatment by the citing sources in general terms. It is incumbent on the researcher to review citing sources with any negative treatment to assess the impact of the citing source on the cited source. A citing source might not overrule a case, but it might criticize or question or distinguish the source to such a degree that it significantly undermines any precedential value the case might have in the future.

So, how do you know you have good law? Ideally, you will know you have good law when you have (1) updated in the source in which you are researching, such as checking the pocket part or supplement to a print source; (2) properly updated on Shepard's or KeyCite, preferably online; (3) seen the sources on which you are relying citing to others of your sources; and (4) looked at some of the more recent cases decided on your issue, if available, to ensure that older cases on which you are relying accurately state the law.

IV. Post Script: A Note About Shepardizing in Print

Shepard's Citations are the most widely used citators in print. If you must update in a print Shepard's, consult the instructions on Shepardizing, available at www.lexisnexis.com/shepards-citations/printsupport/shepardize_print.pdf, or follow the instructions on how to Shepardize in the front of Shepard's books for guidance.

The key to properly Shepardizing in print is locating the right books for the job. Shepard's are published for cite checking cases, statutes, and rules from each state; federal cases, statutes, and regulations; select law reviews; restatements; patents; and ALRs. You will need to locate the correct citator, then collect all of the books and supplements that must be consulted to properly update using that citator. These supplements are not cumulative, which means that you will have to consult multiple supplements to complete updating. A box printed on the front of each supplement identifies its coverage and the books your library should contain to complete updating. Once you have located and collected the proper books, you are ready to begin Shepardizing. The front of every Shepard's volume contains information explaining the various parts of the Shepard's result, which can be overwhelming to the novice researcher without this information.

Chapter 9

Finding and Updating Secondary Sources

Secondary sources summarize, explain, interpret, or comment on the law. Unlike primary sources, which are *the law*, secondary sources are *not the law*, regardless of how persuasive they might be. They are written by lawyers, law professors, law students, and judges who are not acting in a lawmaking capacity when they write these materials.

Most researchers are familiar with secondary sources in non-legal research contexts. Some of these secondary sources include dictionaries, encyclopedias, periodicals, and other reference books. These same types of sources are written in the legal context to assist researchers; these secondary legal sources are the focus of this chapter. Other types of secondary legal sources covered here are *American Law Reports*, looseleaf services, restatements, uniform laws, model codes, CLE materials, form books, and jury instructions.

I. Why Consult Secondary Sources?

Secondary sources can be helpful to researchers in a number of ways: (1) to provide background and an overview on an issue or area of law; (2) as finding tools to assist with identifying relevant primary sources; (3) as persuasive authority when no primary authority exists or when the researcher is arguing for a change in the law or a new interpretation of the law; and (4) as a tool to keep a researcher current in a changing area of law.

First, when a researcher is unfamiliar with an area of law or a topic or issue within an area of law, a secondary source can be a great place to begin research. Secondary sources can identify, explain, and define relevant concepts, and they can alert the researcher to potential issues that should be considered or that may arise. These sources also provide the researcher with additional search terms.

Next, secondary sources may lead the researcher to other relevant sources, both primary and secondary. Some secondary sources, like law review articles and treatises, are heavily footnoted; almost every statement written is supported by citation to other sources. Thus, the researcher can use these footnotes to generate a list of citations to additional sources to review. These footnotes may include citations to cases, statutes, and rules, among other things.

The researcher may also learn what sources are valued by the courts and scholars working in the particular area of law. For example, a researcher working on a federal jurisdiction question may learn from a law review article that a federal statute exists on the issue and may find citations to many federal cases and some well respected treatises. On the other hand, a researcher working on an environmental law issue, such as toxic emissions, may learn that the area of law is controlled by federal regulations, in addition to federal statutes.

Third, secondary sources may serve as persuasive authority for a researcher (1) advocating a change in the law, (2) working in a jurisdiction without relevant primary authority, or (3) seeking interpretations of similar laws from other jurisdictions when the governing primary authority has not yet been interpreted to cover the issue presented in the jurisdiction. In Louisiana, the civil law methodology directs courts to look to *doctrine*, among other things, as persuasive authority when primary authority does not directly address the issue before the court or when interpreting primary authority.[1] Doctrine refers to scholarly writing, which is usually presented in legal trea-

---

1. "Doctrinal interpretation of codal provisions remains today an essential component of the civil law tradition." Kathryn Venturatos Lorio, *The Louisiana Civil Law Tradition: Archaic or Prophetic in the Twenty-First Century?*, 63 La. L. Rev. 1, 22 (2002).

tises, books, and legal periodicals. See Louisiana Lagniappe 9-1, regarding a resurgence of the use of doctrine in Louisiana.

Fourth, secondary sources keep researchers current. Secondary sources in this category are like newsletters, providing frequent updates in rapidly changing areas of law. For example, a secondary source published weekly could analyze a recently enacted statute or an important judicial decision that has broad implications.

II. The Persuasive Value of Secondary Sources

Secondary sources vary in their persuasiveness. A source's persuasiveness depends to a great extent on who wrote it, the type of source in which it is published, where it is published, when it is published, and whether it has been cited as authority in the past.

Who. A source is considered more persuasive when it is written by an author who has a reputation for being a scholar in the field or on the issue. Further, a source that is written by a judge or a law professor will be considered more persuasive than a piece that is written by a law student.

What. Certain types of sources are considered more persuasive than others. Additionally, the more specific the source is at addressing the researcher's issue and his jurisdiction's law, the more persuasive the source will be. Thus, law review articles and treatises on particular topics are typically considered to be more persuasive than legal dictionary entries and legal encyclopedia articles. The latter two sources are general in nature. Further, sources addressing a particular jurisdiction's law are more persuasive than general sources.

Where. Among sources, certain publications are relied upon more than others, often because of a combination of the other factors listed here. For example, the *Restatement (Second) of Torts* is a secondary source that is often consulted by common law courts on tort issues. Among law reviews, some literature exists to indicate that certain law reviews are cited by the courts more often than others. On issues involving Louisiana law, the law reviews from Louisiana law schools and the *Louisiana Civil Law Treatise* series tend to carry weight with Louisiana courts. See Tables 9-2 and 9-3 for a list of these publications.

Louisiana Lagniappe 9-1.

Doctrine in Louisiana Law

In 1937, Louisiana courts and scholars were jolted when a young Louisiana law professor wrote, "Louisiana is today a common law state." His article touched off what many civilian scholars have referred to as a *renaissance of the civil law*. In the wake of the article, Louisiana law schools reformed their curricula to include more courses on the civil law, Louisiana law professors and judges began writing more articles and books on civil law topics, and the Louisiana legislature created the Louisiana State Law Institute. The Law Institute published English translations of French legal commentary so that these works could be consulted by Louisiana lawyers, judges, and scholars. Judges encouraged lawyers and other judges to ground their arguments in the code whenever possible, and judges began to rely upon and cite to French and Spanish authorities to assist in interpreting Louisiana law. J.-R. Trahan, *The Continuing Influence of* le Droit Civil *and* el Derecho Civil *in the Private Law of Louisiana*, 63 La. L. Rev. 1019, 1054–55 (2003).

When. As is true with most sources, persuasiveness will be influenced by how current or up to date a source is kept. Many secondary sources are kept up to date with pocket parts and supplements. Law reviews are not updated in this way, but articles may be checked using Shepard's and KeyCite, which will indicate any sources in which they have been cited.

Citation Record. A source's citation record or history may influence its persuasiveness. If courts have looked to a source in the past, the researcher will have evidence that it is respected by the courts. A writer introducing a persuasive authority should consider including a reference to a citation record if one exists. For example, when introducing information that the writer has retrieved from a treatise, the writer can increase the source's persuasive value by pointing out that the treatise has been cited often by the courts or commentators on the particular point or issue.

III. Types of Secondary Sources and the Process for Researching Them

The process for researching secondary sources varies depending on the source. A general outline is provided in Table 9-1.

Table 9-1. Outline for Researching Secondary Sources

1. Search the library's catalog for the location of relevant secondary sources, or search the database list on an online service.

2. Use your search terms in the index or table of contents of a print secondary source, or run a search in an online database.

3. Find the relevant information in the secondary sources in print or online, being sure to check main volumes and pocket parts or supplements in print sources. Reading the commentary will assist your comprehension of the legal issues. Within the commentary, often in footnotes, find references to primary authority.

4. Update the secondary source, if possible.

5. Read and update the primary authority.

A. Legal Periodicals

1. Overview

Most researchers are familiar with researching in periodicals. The researcher uses search terms in an index to locate articles that address the research issue. Research in legal periodicals is similar.

Legal periodicals are usually referred to as *law reviews* or *law journals*. The pieces published in law reviews and journals include articles or essays authored by law professors, lawyers, and judges, and comments, case notes, and notes authored by law students. Articles, essays, and comments usually focus on a discrete legal issue that the author analyzes in depth. Case notes or notes report on and sometimes comment on recently decided cases. Articles, comments, case notes, and notes are typically heavily footnoted, which is especially helpful to the researcher.

Most law schools publish one or more journals that are edited by student editors. These students have been selected for law review membership because of their high ranking in their law school classes or because of their performance in a writing competition held by the law review. Other law journals, both law school sponsored and non-law school sponsored, are edited by boards made up of lawyers, law professors, and judges.

Many law school journals are considered general journals because they publish pieces on a variety of legal topics; some law schools also publish specialty journals that are dedicated to a particular legal subject. Subject-specific law journals are also published by professional organizations of lawyers and law professors. Table 9-2 provides a list of the journals published by or in conjunction with the law schools in Louisiana. The first journal listed for each school is a general journal, while the remaining journals are subject-specific journals.

Another type of legal periodical is a *bar journal*, which differs from the law journal or law review discussed above primarily in the focus and depth of its pieces. Bar journals are published by bar associations, such as the Louisiana State Bar Association, which publishes the *Louisiana Bar Journal*, and the American Bar Association, which publishes the *ABA Journal*. Articles published in these journals tend to focus on issues of interest to practicing lawyers. They are shorter in length than the pieces discussed above, and they are not as heavily footnoted. If an article addresses the issue you are researching, it can provide a great start, but these articles will not usually cover all aspects of an issue or provide citations to all of the sources that should be researched. Bar journals are printed in a magazine format, and they include advertisements, discipline reports, information about bar-sponsored events, and other information that is pertinent to members of the particular association.

2. Researching Legal Periodicals

Legal periodicals are individual publications that may have their own indices that can be used to conduct research. However, the legal researcher is rarely interested in restricting a search to the articles of one law journal. Thus, to locate citations to relevant law journal

Table 9-2. Law Journals Published by or at
Law Schools in Louisiana

Louisiana State University Paul M. Hebert Law Center	*Louisiana Law Review*
Loyola University New Orleans College of Law	*Loyola Law Review* *Loyola Maritime Law Journal* *Loyola University New Orleans Journal of Public Interest Law* *Loyola Law and Technology Annual*
Southern University Law Center	*Southern University Law Review*
Tulane Law School	*Tulane Law Review* *Tulane Maritime Law Journal* *Tulane European & Civil Law Forum* *Tulane Environmental Law Journal* *Law & Sexuality* *Tulane Journal of International & Comparative Law* *The Sports Lawyers Journal* *Tulane Journal of Technology & Intellectual Property*

pieces, use an indexing service that combines references to many law journals. Indices are available both in print and online. For the reasons stated below, an online index is almost always the best choice.

The indices available in print are the *Index to Legal Periodicals and Books* (ILPB) and the *Current Law Index* (CLI). Both the ILPB and the CLI consist of non-cumulative, annual hardbound volumes, which first appear in softbound pamphlets. The ILPB for a given year first appears as a series of softbound pamphlets that cover months and then quarters, then it finally appears as an annual hardbound volume. The ILPB, which was originally titled the *Index to Legal Periodicals*, can be searched by looking up either a subject or an author's last name in one combined index. This index is especially helpful for finding older articles because it includes citations to articles published as far back as 1908. The ILPB table of cases and the table of statutes are also helpful for locating articles discussing particular cases and statutes.

Publication of the CLI began in 1980. Researchers may conduct searches in the CLI by looking up a subject, case name, statute, or author/title, each of which is found in its own part of the index.

Entries in both the ILPB and the CLI include citation information for articles and may include cross references to other subjects and the names of articles. Make a list of potential articles and locate the journal articles in print or online. For example, a researcher who is referred to 51 Loy. L. Rev. 35 by one of these indices will locate the *Loyola Law Review* on the shelves of the library, locate volume 51, and turn to page 35. The other option is for the researcher to use an online service such as Westlaw or LexisNexis and use the *Find by citation* or *Get a Document* features to retrieve the article by entering the citation. Be aware that these online services do not include every law journal article. If you are unable to locate an article on one service, either try the other service or retrieve the article in print. Additionally, some journals now publish online, which you could determine by conducting a simple search using a search engine like Google or Yahoo!

Searching for law journal articles electronically can be a more efficient use of research time than searching in the non-cumulative print indices. Several options are available to do this. First, the CLI and the ILPB both have electronic products to which law libraries may subscribe. LegalTrac is a CD-ROM product that law libraries may purchase to facilitate the use of the CLI. Law libraries may devote a computer terminal to LegalTrac or may otherwise make it available on library computers. The benefit of using LegalTrac is that it is cumulative, meaning that you may search in one place for all indexed journal articles rather than having to search in annual volumes of the CLI. LegalTrac is updated monthly. Additionally, the ILPB is available electronically through a subscription to the online version, which is found at www.hwwilson.com.

Another online product that allows the researcher to search the full text of many law journal articles is HeinOnline, available at www.heinonline.org. To search the HeinOnline database, a user must have a subscription, which many law school libraries have. This database seems to be regularly expanded to include more journals and more articles. Notably, this database provides links to the articles, which appear in the same format as they do in the printed journals.

A researcher may also search for law journal articles using Westlaw and LexisNexis, which both have databases devoted to legal periodicals. Choose the proper database, then type in search terms, which will allow the full-text searching of all articles found in the database. You will retrieve a list of articles that includes the titles of the articles, citation information, and a relevant passage from the article. You can then print the list of citations to locate the articles in the printed journals. Alternatively, you can click on articles in the list one at a time to review their introductions or the parts of the articles that are most relevant to determine whether the articles are worth printing or downloading for a more careful review. Finally, Google Scholar[2] allows researchers to identify relevant articles in law journals (as well as judicial opinions). Search by author, date, and publication. The search engine links to other sources, including HeinOnline and JSTOR,[3] which provide the text of the articles in PDF format.

B. Legal Treatises and Other Books

1. Overview

A treatise is a scholarly legal publication that is focused on a particular subject matter. A treatise may consist of multiple volumes or a single volume. Treatises often provide a review and analysis of an area of law, a discussion of issues that frequently arise in an area of law, and a discussion of and citations to pertinent cases and statutes. The discussions of issues are usually more focused than discussions in general legal encyclopedias, and they are more heavily footnoted. Treatises are usually divided into discrete sections that are indexed so that the researcher is able to use parts of the treatise without having to read the entire treatise.

---

2. The address is http://scholar.google.com.
3. The address is www.jstor.org.

The value of a good treatise is primarily in the analysis, information, and citations it provides. Further, the reputation of a treatise author and the reputation of the quality of the work will sometimes elevate its value such that courts may turn to it and cite it with approval. For example, on issues of Louisiana law, the *Louisiana Civil Law Treatise* series is well respected, as is the *Civil Law Translation* series, which provides translations of well known French treatises for the researcher who desires further insight into civil law topics. On issues of federal civil procedure, *Federal Practice and Procedure* and *Moore's Federal Practice* are treatises that have been cited by courts due in part to the authors of these works and to the consistent high quality of the books.

Louisiana Lagniappe 9-2.

The Value of Doctrine

Commenting on the value of cases and the value of doctrine, Marcel Planiol, well known French commentator and Honorary Professor of the Faculty of Law of Paris, wrote in the early 1900s: "Let us take case law for what it is, a customary law of recent formation. And let us teach it as such, with our comments. The real task of 'doctrine,' and the only one that is useful, is to help fill in the gaps; to advise as to new questions which have not yet been worked out in the adjudged cases." Marcel Planiol & George Ripert, *Traite Elementaire de Droit Civil* 20 (La. St. L. Inst. Trans., 1959).

---

a. Multi-Volume Treatises

Treatises exist in various formats. The *Louisiana Civil Law Treatise* series is a comprehensive, multi-volume work that addresses the various topics covered by the civil law as well as civil and criminal procedure. The volumes are written by Louisiana law scholars, including practitioners, judges, and law professors. The treatise series provides (1) in-depth discussion and analysis of areas of law, (2) citations to both primary and secondary authorities pertaining to the subject matters, and (3) forms and checklists relevant to the area of law. See Table 9-3 for a list of the titles within the series.

The *Civil Law Translations* series is a multi-volume set of well known French civil law treatises and articles, which have been translated from French to English. This series was made possible through the Louisiana State Law Institute. The *Civil Law Translation* series

Table 9-3. *Louisiana Civil Law Treatise* Titles

Civil Procedure (vol. 1)	*Workers' Compensation Law and Practice* (vols. 13–14)
Civil Procedure—Special Proceedings (vol. 1A)	*Insurance Law and Practice* (vol. 15)
Property (vol. 2)	*Matrimonial Regimes* (vol. 16)
Personal Servitudes (vol. 3)	*Criminal Jury Instructions and Procedures* (vol. 17)
Predial Servitudes (vol. 4)	*Civil Jury Instructions* (vol. 18)
The Law of Obligations (vols. 5–6)	*Evidence and Proof* (vol. 19)
Business Organizations (vols. 7–8)	*Legislative Law and Procedure* (vol. 20)
Limited Liability Companies and Partnerships (vol. 9)	*Louisiana Lawyering* (vol. 21)
Successions and Donations (vol. 10)	*Louisiana Summary Judgment and Termination Motions* (vol. 22)
Trusts (vol. 11)	*Louisiana Motions in Limine* (vol. 23)
Tort Law (vol. 12)	*Sales* (vol. 24)

contains translated commentary by Aubry and Rau on Obligations, Property, Testamentary Successions and Gratuitous Dispositions, Intestate Successions, and Prescription. It also includes a translation of the work of Francois Geny on interpreting law and a translation of Marcel Planiol and George Ripert's *Treatise on Civil Law.* This series is helpful in doing historical research as well as in trying to determine the proper interpretation of a Louisiana code article that is based on French law. See Louisiana Lagniappe 9-2 on the value of doctrine.

b. Monographs

Single books or monographs on legal topics are also published. The usefulness of these types of books will vary widely, depending on how well they are indexed, how often they are updated, how broad or narrow the book's focus is, and whether the author has supported statements with citations to primary and other secondary sources. These books will usually be found in the library grouped together by subject matter.

c. Hornbooks, Nutshells, Deskbooks, and Practice Guides

In addition to a single book on a topic written by an individual author or authors, some recurring types of books on legal topics are hornbooks, *Nutshells*, deskbooks, and practice guides. Hornbooks and *Nutshells* are books that provide a general overview of an area of law. They are marketed to law students as study aides. They are usually not jurisdiction-specific so their value in researching the law of a specific jurisdiction is limited. Hornbooks usually include more citations to primary sources than *Nutshells*. *Nutshells* are a series of paperback books published by West that serve primarily to bring law students up to speed on an area of law. For the researcher, these books may be helpful to provide background information or an overview of an area of law before the researcher begins more specific research.

Deskbooks and practice guides are geared to assisting practicing lawyers in a particular area of law, although their formats vary. Unlike hornbooks and *Nutshells*, they usually focus on the law and procedures of specific jurisdictions. They often include such things as explanations of the law and how it has been interpreted, checklists, forms, unannotated versions of rules of procedure, evidence rules, and court rules. Deskbooks tend to be more practical, rather than analytical or theoretical. Examples of deskbooks and practice guides on Louisiana practice are listed in Table 9-4.

Because different fields of law have different needs, deskbooks and practice guides include information and tools specifically useful for

Table 9-4. Deskbooks and Practice Guides

Deskbooks:
Handbook on Louisiana Evidence Law
Handbook on Louisiana Family Law
Louisiana's Children's Code Handbook
Louisiana Handbook of Statutory Criminal Law and Procedure
Louisiana Sentencing Guidelines Manual

Practice Guides from the *Louisiana Practice* Series:
Estate Planning in Louisiana
Louisiana Civil Appellate Procedure Handbook
Louisiana Civil Practice Forms
Louisiana Civil Pretrial Procedure
Louisiana Civil Procedure
Louisiana Civil Trial Procedure
Louisiana Construction Law
Louisiana Corporations
Louisiana Criminal Trial Practice
Louisiana Divorce
Louisiana Elements of an Action
Louisiana Employment Law
Louisiana Environmental Compliance Handbook
Louisiana Evidence
Louisiana Notary Handbook
Louisiana Personal Injury
Louisiana Real Estate Transactions
Louisiana Secured Transactions
Trial Handbook for Louisiana Lawyers

that area of law. Therefore, in addition to the text, many of the volumes contain appendices of statutory and regulatory materials; useful forms related to the material to serve as a guide in creating forms tailored to the client's need; and author commentary to facilitate the researcher's understanding of the subject matter. Similar deskbooks and practice guides exist in most states.

2. Researching Treatises and Other Books

As in researching books in other disciplines, the first step to researching legal treatises and books is identifying the titles in which you will search. Sometimes you will be familiar with the titles covering a particular area of law because of experience in the field or because of other research that has identified the titles. When you are unfamiliar with the treatises or books available on a particular area of law, consult a law librarian, a lawyer with experience in the area of law, or a library catalog to find out what treatises or books are available. After identifying titles, you are ready to use search terms in the index or table of contents to the treatise or book to find specific volumes, sections, and pages that seem most relevant to the issue. Then locate those specific portions of the source and review them to determine their value.

Treatises and books are updated in various ways. Consider whether you are looking at the most recent edition of a treatise or book and whether there are any supplements or pocket parts or inserts to the treatise or book.

An example of researching a specific topic in the *Louisiana Civil Law Treatise* follows. Assume you have a question concerning insurance coverage of rental vehicles under Louisiana law. Begin by pulling the *Insurance Law and Practice* volume of the *Louisiana Civil Law Treatise*. In this treatise, each of the volumes has its own table of contents and index. The index is an easy place to start because the topics are in alphabetical order. Using the search term *rental vehicles*, you will quickly find that rental vehicles are covered in three different sections of the treatise volume. Look at each of these sections to determine their relevance.

The section that is most relevant, §61 of the volume, is entitled *Vehicles insured–Temporary substitute automobiles*. See Figure 9-1. This section gives explanatory text as well as footnotes to pertinent cases. The *Research References* section guides you to other useful sources. The final step is to check the pocket part of the treatise. This is done by opening the pocket part to §61, which lists footnote 18 along with a new case on the subject matter. You now know that this case is the most recent case on point as of the publishing date of the

Figure 9-1. Excerpt from *Louisiana Civil Law Treatise*

AUTOMOBILE LIABILITY INSURANCE   § 61

longer the owner may be ground for reformation or estoppel.[6]

§ 61 Vehicles insured — Temporary substitute automobiles

Research References

West's Key Number Digest, Insurance ⊙═ 2658

C.J.S., Insurance §§ 56, 1041, 1590, 1674

Policies extend the definition of the owned or covered auto to include a "temporary substitute automobile." The policy definition of a temporary substitute automobile vary and therefore should be read carefully. The definition contained in the 1974 Basic Automobile Liability Policy is as follows:

> "Temporary substitute automobile" means an automobile not owned by the named insured or any resident of the same household, while temporarily used with the permission of the owner as a substitute for an owned automobile when withdrawn from normal use for servicing or repair or because of breakdown, loss or destruction.

The burden of proof on a person asserting coverage is to establish all of the elements required by the definition of temporary substitute automobile.[1] The 1956 Family Automobile Policy contained no exception for a vehicle owned by the named insured or others. The 1958 Family Automobile Policy added an exception for an automobile owned by the named insured only,[2] which is also the exception in the Personal Auto Policy.[3] Other policy forms also exclude an automobile owned by any resident of the same household as the named insured. When excepted from the definition, the courts have enforced the policy language by not classifying automobiles owned by the named insured,[4] or any resident of the same

---

[6]Thibeau v. LeBlanc, 198 So. 2d 707 (La. Ct. App. 1st Cir. 1967)(estoppel); Maggio v. State Farm Mut. Auto. Ins. Co., 123 So. 2d 901 (La. Ct. App. 1st Cir. 1960), writ denied. See § 5, supra.

[Section 61]

[1]Normand v. Hertz Corp., 254 La. 1075, 229 So. 2d 104 (1969)(overruled by, Jones v. Breaux, 289 So. 2d 110 (La. 1974)) (overruled on other grounds by Jones v. Breaux, 289 So. 2d 110 (La. 1974).

[2]For discussion of this modification, *See* Fontenot v. State Farm Mut. Ins. Co., 119 So. 2d 588 (La. Ct. App.

1st Cir. 1960).

[3]*See* Appendix A, infra.

[4]Robinson v. Heard, 809 So. Sd 943 (La. 2002). In the name of his sole proprietorship, Mike Robinson Enterprises, plaintiff owned a truck insured by Interstate under a commercial policy with UM coverage. Plaintiff also owned a vehicle insured by Interstate under a personal auto policy without UM coverage. When the accident occurred, plaintiff was using his personal vehicle in his business because his commercial truck had a flat tire. Reversing the First Circuit, the Court found that the personal vehicle did not qualify as a temporary substitute auto

---

Source: 15 William Shelby McKenzie & H. Alston Johnson III, *Louisiana Civil Law Treatise, Insurance Law and Practice* § 61 (2006). Reprinted with permission of Thomson Reuters.

pocket part. If there were no §61 in the pocket part, you would know that no additional information had been added to the information in the text.

Some treatises and books are available online through LexisNexis and Westlaw. As with print research, you will need to identify the source or sources you would like to search, although online you will be able to run a search in several databases or sources at one time. Type in search terms to receive a list of possible sections that satisfy your query with short excerpts from the sections and citation information. Then click on each section that interests you and assess its value, or print the list of citations to use in the print sources. If you are looking at a source through an online service, you should find information about how the source is updated. Sometimes the source will be automatically updated at a regular interval and sometimes a link to updates will be provided.

C. Legal Encyclopedias

1. Overview

Legal encyclopedias provide a general overview of law pertaining to a variety of legal topics, with references to cases and other practice materials provided in footnotes. Because of the general nature of the discussions in most legal encyclopedias, they serve best as sources of background information and as finding tools to assist with identifying relevant primary sources. Rarely will it be appropriate to cite a legal encyclopedia discussion, even as persuasive authority on a point of law.

Currently, two sets of legal encyclopedias discuss American law: *American Jurisprudence 2d*, commonly referred to as Am Jur 2d, and *Corpus Juris Secundum*, commonly referred to as CJS. These encyclopedias provide footnotes to federal and state cases from across the United States, but they do not focus on any specific jurisdiction. Rather, they summarize law in the United States and may identify trends in the law and different approaches taken by courts. Additionally, Am Jur 2d provides references to the *American Law Reports* series and to other texts published by its publisher, Lawyers Co-operative, and CJS provides references to West topics and key numbers and other West publications.

In addition to Am Jur 2d and CJS, some encyclopedias are state-specific. For example, *Florida Jurisprudence 2d* summarizes Florida state law, and *Texas Jurisprudence 2d* summarizes Texas law. However, the majority of states, including Louisiana, do not have their own legal encyclopedia. (But see references to some Louisiana-specific materials in the previous section on treatises and other books.)

2. Researching in a Legal Encyclopedia

After determining which encyclopedias are available, begin research by selecting a topic in the encyclopedia or turning to the encyclopedia's index with a list of search terms. Most multi-volume sets of encyclopedias are organized alphabetically by topic, with a list of topics printed at the beginning of the set. Additionally, an analysis or outline of what is included within a topic is provided at the start of each topic discussion. Once you have identified potentially relevant topics and sections either by using the index or by using the analysis at the start of a topic, read the identified sections, looking for discussions relevant to the legal issue and for citations to primary sources or other research sources. Check for any supplements or pocket parts to the publication to update the research.

Legal encyclopedias are also available online using Westlaw and LexisNexis. Both services include Am Jur 2d and some state encyclopedias. Westlaw also includes CJS. On Westlaw, the database identifiers for legal encyclopedias are listed in the Westlaw directory under *Forms, Treatises, CLE, and Other Practice Material.* On LexisNexis, the database identifiers are listed under *Legal Sources*, then *Secondary Legal*, then *Jurisprudence, ALR & Encyclopedias.* You may search on both services using terms and connectors or natural language searches or by browsing the encyclopedia's table of contents.

Finally, some free online services offer encyclopedias that are less reliable than traditional encyclopedias and do not provide sophisticated searching. However, these services can provide useful information at the early stages of research. For example, the Legal Information Institute (L.I.I.) hosted by Cornell University provides an online encyclopedia/dictionary called Wex.[4] It is a wiki website, meaning that the content is provided by volunteer contributors. Its list of search terms is extensive, and it also provides a search box for keyword searching.

D. *American Law Reports*

1. Overview

The *American Law Reports*, known as ALR, is a unique publication because it contains both primary and secondary authority. It is discussed in the chapter on secondary authority because its value is not in its publication of cases, but in its extensive commentary and discussion of the legal issues raised in those cases.

ALR publishes cases from American jurisdictions that it deems to address significant legal issues. Each case is published in its entirety, accompanied by an *annotation* that includes a full discussion of a point of law referenced in the case. The annotation provides citations to cases from multiple American jurisdictions as well as to other secondary authorities. Headnotes preceding the cases, which are similar to the headnotes in West publications, are written by Lawyers Co-operative editors and are tied to ALR digests, not West digests. At the start of the annotation, the researcher will find a table of contents, cross references to other relevant Lawyers Co-operative publications, a subject index, and a *Table of Jurisdictions Represented* or mentioned in the annotation. An introduction identifies the scope of the annotation and provides citations to related ALR annotations. This list of related annotations can prove particularly helpful to lead to annotations that may be even more relevant for the research project.

A relevant annotation can be valuable at the early stages of research because it provides a full discussion and analysis of the issue it is addressing and it identifies differences among American jurisdictions as to their treatment of the issue. Also, it collects relevant cases from all American jurisdictions, providing citations to both binding and persuasive primary authority. Each annotation is updated to keep up with changes in the law on the legal issue addressed.

---

4. The website address is http://topics.law.cornell.edu/wex.

The ALR has been published in eight series: ALR, ALR2d, ALR3d, ALR4th, ALR5th, ALR6th, ALR Fed., and ALR Fed. 2d. The more modern series, from ALR3d forward, have more features and are similar to each other in format. ALR, ALR2d, and some early volumes in the ALR3d series include both state and federal law issues. Beginning in 1969, all federal law issues were moved to a new series, ALR Fed., and only state law issues were addressed in the later numbered editions of the publication. Each series has multiple volumes organized by volume number.

2. Researching in the ALRs

Researching to find a relevant ALR annotation can be done both in print and online. In print, if you are researching an issue of state law, begin with search terms in the *ALR Quick Index*, which covers annotations found in the ALR3d through the ALR6th series. If your research deals exclusively with federal law, begin in the *ALR Federal Quick Index*. The *ALR Index to Annotations*, which includes references to annotations found in all series from the ALR2d series on, is a more comprehensive index for locating annotations addressing both state and federal law. The *ALR First Series Quick Index* indexes the annotations in the first series. This index should not be consulted unless references in the newer editions of the series do not exist.

Researching with an ALR index is similar to researching with other indices. Search for key terms, which will lead to citations to annotations related to those terms. Each index entry includes a brief statement identifying the issue addressed in the annotation in addition to its citation. The index also provides cross references to other terms. Be careful to note the series designation when writing down the annotation citations. Additionally, consult the pocket part to the index to find references to additional annotations.

To search for annotations referencing specific statutes, use the *Table of Laws, Rules, and Regulations* located in the back of the index.

Another method to find relevant annotations is to use the *ALR Digest*, which includes references to annotations in the ALR3d, ALR4th, ALR5th, ALR6th, ALR Fed., and ALR Fed. 2d. The *Digest* separates the law into topics and subtopics and gives short summaries of the annotations relating to these topics. While the *Digest* may be a helpful tool for the researcher who is having trouble finding annotations relevant to his topic through the index, the index is generally the better place to begin.

You can also locate citations to annotations online using Lexis-Nexis and Westlaw. Both of these services provide databases that allow searching the full text of annotations for key words.

Once you have citations, turn to the corresponding annotations in the volumes or open that portion of the database. Skim the material at the beginning of the annotation, including the introduction, to ensure that the annotation is relevant before reading the entire entry.

The ALR series is updated in several ways: (1) by new editions; (2) by pocket parts to supplement the volumes, the indices, and the digests; and (3) by the *Annotation History Table*, which is found in the index. It is important to check pocket parts and the *Annotation History Table* before relying on the annotation printed in the volume because sometimes entire annotations or sections of annotations are superseded by new ones to keep abreast of changes in the law. The pocket part will indicate what changes have been made to an annotation.[5] Online, the ALR material is updated weekly by the addition of relevant cases, and the annotations may be updated using Shepard's and KeyCite.

E. Restatements

Restatements are appropriately named because they summarize or *re-state* American common law on a subject. The American Law Institute (ALI) has published restatements in a variety of fields, including: Agency, Conflicts of Law, Contracts, Foreign Relations, Judgments, Law Governing Lawyers, Property, Restitution, Security, Suretyship

---

5. ALR and ALR2d are updated a bit differently. ALR2d is updated through the use of *Later Case Service* volumes, and ALR is updated through the *ALR Blue Book of Supplemental Decisions*.

and Guaranty, Torts, Trusts, and Unfair Competition. Most of these restatements are in their second or third revision, which is designated in the publication's title, such as the *Restatement (Second) of Torts*. Because of their focus on common law, restatements can be particularly helpful when researching the law of common law American jurisdictions on one of the subjects for which a restatement has been published. Further, restatements have some limited value when researching Louisiana law. Louisiana courts have recognized the persuasive value of restatements in some areas of law, such as tort law.[6]

Restatements present common law rules, sometimes including both majority and minority rules and interpretations. Additionally, restatements provide commentary on the rules, illustrations suggesting how the rules should be applied, and citations to and brief summaries of cases in which the restatement section has been interpreted.

Although the common law rules presented in the restatements often look like statutes, they are not statutes. They can only become primary authority if a court or a legislature adopts them as such. If the courts of a jurisdiction have adopted a restatement as law, the researcher can use the restatement effectively to locate persuasive authority from other jurisdictions cited in the restatement's discussion.

You can search for available restatements using a library's catalog by searching for the general subject being researched or for the word *restatement*. Once the restatement is located, use search terms in the restatement's index or table of contents to locate relevant sections. Relevant sections of the restatement will include the rule, comments, and illustrations. The corresponding Appendix volumes of the restatement will provide information about citing cases.

You can also search for applicable restatement sections using Westlaw and LexisNexis and appropriate search terms. A search can be run in a restatement database on both services. Additionally, you can run a search for restatement references in other databases, such as databases including cases or journal articles.

---

6. *See, e.g., Nicholas v. Allstate Ins. Co.*, 765 So. 2d 1017, 1021 n.4 (La. 2000).

F. Uniform Laws and Model Codes

Uniform laws and *model codes*, such as the *Uniform Commercial Code* and the *Model Penal Code*, are proposed statutes that can be adopted by legislatures. The National Conference of Commissioners on United States Laws (NCCUSL) drafts uniform laws on legal issues that it determines would benefit from uniformity of law across states, such as business law and family law. The NCCUSL and the ALI draft model codes with the intent of reforming existing laws, such as the *Model Penal Code* and the *Model Code of Evidence.* While restatements simply purport to summarize existing common law in a statute-like form, uniform laws and model codes present proposed statutes with the intent that they will be enacted into states' codes.

Prior to adoption by a state legislature, uniform laws and model codes do not have the authority of law; they are secondary authorities. When they are adopted, often legislatures will modify the uniform law or the model code to some degree, making it imperative that the researcher locate the exact provision that was enacted into law by the legislature.

The Louisiana legislature has adopted several uniform laws, including parts of the Uniform Commercial Code, the Uniform Child Custody Jurisdiction Act, and the Uniform Probate Code Act. A listing of uniform laws that have been adopted by the Louisiana legislature and their corresponding Louisiana citations may be found at www.lawsource.com/also/usa.cgi?usm&la. Additionally, links to state statutes corresponding to uniform laws are provided at www.law.cornell.edu/uniform.

Researching in uniform laws and model codes may be useful for gathering information on how to interpret a state law that is based on one of these sources. In that situation, the researcher will probably have a citation to the uniform law or the model code that is provided with the state law. He will locate the applicable uniform law or model code using a library catalog or an online research service.

These publications may also prove helpful to the researcher who is advocating a change in existing state law. The researcher can search a library catalog under the relevant subject or for *uniform laws* or *model codes* to identify available publications. Then, he will use search terms in the index or the table of contents of the publication to locate potentially helpful sections. A similar search can also be run on Lexis-Nexis and Westlaw.

In addition to the text of the proposed statutes, uniform laws and model codes publications may provide explanatory notes on the proposed statutes that were written by the authors. They may also identify jurisdictions that have adopted the proposed statutes, provide cross references to other secondary authorities that have discussed the proposed or adopted statutes, and provide citations to and summaries of cases in which the proposed or adopted statutes have been discussed.

G. Continuing Legal Education Materials

Continuing Legal Education (CLE) is a requirement for maintaining good standing as an attorney in Louisiana and in most other states. CLE materials consist of the handouts distributed by the CLE instructors, who are generally practitioners, judges, or law professors. The CLE materials usually focus on a particular legal subject matter and can be useful as an introductory tool to a specific matter. While CLE materials are probably not the best place to acquire all relevant research or even to begin research, they can be useful research tools because of their practical emphasis.

The Louisiana State Bar Association produces CLE materials, as do various law schools and legal organizations. Additionally, the Practising Law Institute (PLI) and the American Law Institute-American Bar Association (ALI-ABA) are two of the largest CLE material publishers whose materials can be accessed in print and online.

One way to find CLE materials is to locate publications on the subject you are researching using the library catalog. CLE materials are catalogued and shelved by subject in most law libraries. Once you have identified the location, review the materials available, especially looking for good discussions of relevant legal issues that are supported by citations to primary authorities and other secondary authorities.

Another way to locate CLE materials is online. The ALI-ABA, the ABA, and the PLI publish CLE materials on their websites. CLE materials may also be located on Lexis and Westlaw. On Lexis, search in Secondary Legal" under "CLE Materials." On Westlaw, search in the database "Treatises, CLEs, and Other Practice Materials."

CLE materials should serve only as an introductory tool on a particular matter of law or as a tool for learning about a new development in the law. They are rarely cited in judicial opinions or scholarly publications. Moreover, because most CLE materials are not regularly updated, you should update any material gathered from these sources.

H. Forms and Jury Instructions

Forms and sample jury instructions are available in most jurisdictions to assist practitioners. The most helpful of these types of documents, from a research standpoint, are annotated forms and instructions that provide citations to authority to support language found in the documents. The annotated documents will lead to primary authorities and other secondary authorities and will also provide the information necessary for assessing the relevance of the form or instruction to the client's case. Forms and sample jury instructions also provide valuable information to the practitioner who is new to how things are done in a particular jurisdiction.

The term *forms* is used to refer to sample legal documents, such as forms for contracts, pleadings, wills, and even client letters. The term *jury instructions* refers to the instructions given by a judge to a jury before the jury is sent to deliberate in a case. Sometimes courts will provide attorneys with suggested jury instructions and give the attorneys an opportunity to voice any objections; sometimes courts will ask the attorneys to propose jury instructions.

What you should remember when using any of these resources is that any document you produce for a client and any instructions you submit to a court must be tailored to your client and your case and to the current, applicable law.

Forms and jury instructions may be found in several different contexts. First, they may be found in books dedicated to forms or jury instructions. Two examples of form books include the *Louisiana Criminal Trial Practice Formulary*[7] and *Louisiana Civil Practice Forms*,[8] which provide forms that are annotated with references to governing law and other secondary authorities. An example of a book focused on jury instructions is part of the *Louisiana Civil Treatise* series, *Criminal Jury Instructions and Procedure*.[9] This book is also annotated.

Second, forms and instructions may be found in practice guides on particular legal topics, along with significant discussion of the law. For example, forms are provided in most of the books published as part of the *Louisiana Practice* series on particular legal topics; this series is discussed in Section II.B.1 of this chapter.

Third, forms are often found with governing rules of procedure and court rules. For example, the *Appendix to the Federal Rules of Civil Procedure* includes forms for documents that are frequently filed with the federal district courts. Fourth, many court websites include forms, and federal appellate courts' websites include links to model and pattern jury instructions, which are used throughout the federal courts.

To determine which publications are available, check a library catalog under the relevant subject matter as well as under the terms *forms* or *jury instructions*. You can check rules of court and procedural rules as well as court websites. Additionally, you can research forms and jury instructions on Westlaw and LexisNexis, which have databases dedicated to forms and jury instructions.

I. Legal Dictionaries

Legal dictionaries, like other dictionaries, define terms and provide information on the proper pronunciation and usage of words. Legal

---

7. Gail Dalton Schlosser, *Louisiana Criminal Trial Practice Formulary* (2d ed. 2000).

8. Susan B. Kohn & Denise M. Pilié, *Louisiana Civil Practice Forms* (2008 ed.).

9. Cheney C. Joseph, Jr. & P. Raymond Lamonica, *Criminal Jury Instructions and Procedure* (2d ed. 2003).

dictionaries focus on legal words and terms of art; they may also include citations to sources from which definitions were obtained.

Legal dictionaries are available in print and online. They should be consulted by researchers who encounter unfamiliar words in their research, but they should not be considered as sources for conducting original legal research. From time to time, a court will reference *Black's Law Dictionary* or some other legal dictionary, but these sources should never be cited as authoritative.

Chapter 10

Online Legal Research

Online research is often necessary for conducting effective and cost-efficient legal research. For the novice researcher who has grown accustomed to using search engines such as Google, Bing, and Yahoo! to locate information, online legal research may appear to be an easy task that can be done relatively quickly. Type a few key terms into these search engines, and watch as the answer to your query is revealed on multiple websites. Unlike other online research, however, legal research requires a high level of precision, both in deciding where to search and in constructing searches.

This chapter begins with basic information for conducting legal research online. This introduction will be essential for researchers with less online experience, while providing a quick overview for researchers savvy about online techniques. The chapter then delves into more sophisticated search techniques. This chapter supplements the techniques for researching specific sources online that have been included in the chapters of the book addressing those specific sources. Additionally, Appendix B contains websites of interest to the researcher with a focus on those containing Louisiana law.

I. Overview of Researching Online

The fundamental steps for constructing an effective online search are provided in Table 10-1.

Table 10-1. Steps for Constructing an Effective Online Search

1. Clarify the issue and determine what you hope to find.
2. Choose a site or service.
3. Generate search terms, then modify them with expanders and placeholders.
4. Add connectors.
5. Refine the search based on the results.

A. Clarify the Issue and Determine What You Hope to Find

First, carefully think through the legal issue. Try to write a single sentence that summarizes the question you hope to answer. Remember that the computer is no smarter than you are, and it interprets queries literally.

Also, determine what you hope to find. It is easy for a researcher to become distracted or overwhelmed by search results online because online services often provide results that amount to a search of an entire library. For example, a researcher looking for a statute from a particular state in print will probably search the index to the state statutes, rather than checking all publications in the library. However, online a researcher may be tempted to run a search broadly or may become distracted by sources from other jurisdictions or secondary sources that are often displayed with search results. Know before you go online the authoritative sources in which you expect to find what you are looking for, and narrow your search by database or source when possible. Rarely are researchers looking for everything ever written on a topic; maintain focus on what is authoritative and relevant to your work.

B. Choose a Site or Service

After clarifying the issue, determine which online sites you will use to conduct your search. Consider whether the material you hope to find is available from a free, yet reliable, site. Many resources can be found through the major online directories to free online legal information, including the Library of Congress's Guide to Law Online[1] and Cornell University's Legal Information Institute (L.I.I.)[2] These directories link to the websites of legislatures, courts, and government agencies, as well as other websites.

Google Scholar[3] is another source for legal documents provided free online. It provides access to many law review and journal articles and to many federal and state judicial decisions. The Legal Scholarship Network on Social Science Research Network (S.S.R.N.)[4] provides free access to legal scholarship, as well.

When considering commercial providers, weigh the cost of services like Lexis, Lexis Advance, Westlaw, and WestlawNext against their sophisticated search engines, vast resources, and reliability. LexisNexis and West are the predominant vendors of online legal information, and their search engines and resources are currently more extensive than those of the free services.

Additionally, commercial options exist that are not as expensive as the LexisNexis and West services, but that are also not as extensive in searching capability or in coverage. These options should be considered to keep costs down when they provide access to the sources most relevant to the topic and search being conducted. See Table 10-2 for a list of online commercial legal database providers.

After selecting an online provider, often you must also choose which subset of that provider's resources to use. LexisNexis and Westlaw divide their resources into groups by type of document, topic, and jurisdiction. In LexisNexis, these groups are simply called *sources*. In Westlaw, information is grouped into *databases*.

Both LexisNexis and Westlaw have directories to allow you to browse among the sources and databases that are available for research. Clicking on the *i* next to the name of a source or database will provide information about its scope. Note that the list of sources or

---

1. The address is www.loc.gov/law/help.
2. The address is www.law.cornell.edu.
3. The address is http://scholar.google.com.
4. The address is www.ssrn.com/lsn.

Table 10-2. Websites for Commercial Providers

Provider	Web Address
Bloomberg Law	www.bloomberg.com/solutions/business_solutions/law
Casemaker (free to members of some state bar associations)	www.casemaker.us
Fastcase (free to members of some state bar associations)	www.fastcase.com
LexisNexis	www.lexisnexis.com
Loislaw	www.loislaw.com
VersusLaw	www.versuslaw.com
West	www.westlaw.com

databases shown on a particular page may not include all that are available. On LexisNexis, you may need to click on *View more sources*. On Westlaw, you may need to add more databases to those shown on a particular tab.

Try to restrict each search to the smallest set of sources or databases that will contain the documents needed. Because online databases often correspond to print series, it may be helpful to think of yourself in the stacks of the library when choosing sources or databases. Do you really want to search the contents of every reporter on the second floor, or do you want to search just the *Southern Reporter*? In addition to producing a more focused set of results, smaller databases also tend to be less expensive than their larger counterparts.

C. Generate Search Terms

Generate a comprehensive list of search terms, following the suggestions in Chapter 2. This step is critically important in online research, given the literal nature of search engines. If the author of a particular document does not use the exact term you are searching for, that document will not appear in your results.

In generating a list of terms, include both broad and narrow terms. For example, in a search about driving a motorcycle in a state park, you may want to include not only *motorcycle* but also *motorized vehicle*. Include synonyms and antonyms of search terms whenever possible.

Next, modify the search terms with expanders and placeholders so that a search will find variations of your words. The exclamation point expands words beyond a common root. For example, *employ!* will find employee, employer, employed, employs, employing, etc.

The asterisk serves as a placeholder for an individual letter. Up to three asterisks can be used in a single term. This symbol is helpful when you are not sure which form of the word is used, or when you are not sure of the spelling of a word. For example, the search term *dr*nk* will find drink, drank, and drunk. Place holders are preferable to the expander in some instances. Using an expander on *trad!* with hopes of finding *trade, trading, trades*, etc. will also produce results that include *traditional*. A better search term may be *trad****.

D. Add Connectors

Connectors determine where search terms will be placed in relation to one another in targeted documents. Effective use of connectors is critical in finding relevant authority. Even minimally sophisticated use of the various connectors can make your searches much more effective. Table 10-3 summarizes the most common connectors used on LexisNexis and Westlaw.

Most connectors are the same for the two services. However, two differences can cause some confusion. On LexisNexis, searching alternative terms requires the use of the connector *or*. On Westlaw, a blank space is interpreted as *or*. The second difference concerns phrases or terms of art. LexisNexis reads a blank space as joining words in a phrase. By contrast, to search a phrase on Westlaw, the terms must be enclosed in quotation marks. Examples are shown in Table 10-3. If you type in *negligent homicide* on LexisNexis you will retrieve documents including those terms together as a term of art. However, if you enter the same search on Westlaw, you will retrieve

Table 10-3. Connectors

Meaning of Connector	LexisNexis	Westlaw
or	or *negligent or homicide*	or; alternatively, leave a space between two words *negligent or homicide* *negligent homicide*
and	and *negligent and homicide*	& *negligent & homicide*
term within so many words of another term	w/# *negligent w/3 homicide*	/# *negligent /3 homicide*
term within the same sentence as another term	w/s *negligent w/s homicide*	/s *negligent /s homicide*
term within the same paragraph as another term	w/p *negligent w/p homicide*	/p *negligent /p homicide*
phrase or term of art	no connector needed *negligent homicide*	place quotation marks around the phrase or term of art *"negligent homicide"*

documents containing the word *negligent* or the word *homicide*, probably yielding a large number of irrelevant cases if you are researching the criminal charge of negligent homicide.

E. Refine the Search

With a query of terms and connectors, you can conduct a search. Many of your initial searches might locate either no documents or more than 1,000 documents. With practice, you will learn to craft more precise searches that produce more helpful results.

If a search produces no results, use broader connectors (*e.g.*, search for terms in the same paragraph rather than in the same sentence), use additional alternative terms, or use a larger set of sources or a larger database. If a search produces a long list of results, skim them to see whether they are on point. If the results seem irrelevant, modify or edit the search query by omitting broad terms, using more restrictive connectors, or using a smaller set of sources or databases.

The *FOCUS* feature on LexisNexis and the *Locate* feature on Westlaw can be used to narrow results further. These features allow a researcher to construct a search within a search and produce a subset of the initial search results. These features can be very cost efficient because they do not result in the additional charges of a new search. A good strategy may be to create a broader initial search than you otherwise might and plan to conduct a series of restricting searches on the results.

II. Additional Online Search Techniques

The text below introduces more sophisticated search techniques and offers suggestions for effective and efficient online searching.

A. Segment and Field Searching

Both LexisNexis and Westlaw allow you to search specific parts of documents, such as the date, author, or court. The options are available on drop-down menus. On LexisNexis, these specific parts are called document *segments*; on Westlaw, they are called *fields*. A segment or field term is added to the basic search with an appropriate connector.

A few examples demonstrate the usefulness of segment and field searching. First, in conducting a full-text search, you can ensure that the results directly address your topic by searching the syllabi or synopses of the documents. Because this segment or field summarizes the contents of the document, your terms will appear there only if they are the focus of the document. Thus, the search will weed out documents where your terms are mentioned only in passing or in a footnote. Second, if you know the author of a relevant opinion or article, you can search for her name in the appropriate segment or field, eliminating documents where the person is referred to only tangentially.[5]

B. Natural Language Searching

Natural language search engines allow searches that use a simple question or phrase, as opposed to a series of terms and connectors. These search engines lack the precision of terms and connectors searching, but allow you to construct a search more quickly and intuitively.

Natural language search engines are designed to produce a list of results and to rank the value of the results. These aspects of natural language searching can seem positive after the frustration of terms and connectors searches that returned no results, but several caveats are important. Some hits appear first in result lists simply because sponsors pay for this privilege. Sometimes the best hit from your perspective will be the search engine's fourteenth best match, so skimming through the results is always very important. Furthermore, natural language searching can produce lists of documents that are not very relevant to your research. This may mean that no better matches exist or that the search was not crafted well enough. When conducting the search on the Internet, poor results may mean that this particular search engine did not scan the portion of the Internet that contains the needed documents. On LexisNexis and Westlaw, the natural language programs are set to retrieve a particular number of results. Often that number is 20 or 100, though you can change the default. Again, the fact that the computer returned 100 documents does not mean that those 100 documents are all relevant.

While natural language searching can be very helpful to the novice online researcher, skilled terms and connectors searching will almost always be more powerful and accurate. Law students should take advantage of their unfettered access to LexisNexis and Westlaw by extensively practicing terms and connectors searching. Practitioners can take advantage of free training provided by the commercial providers.

---

5. *See also* Chapter 6, Part III.E, which includes a discussion of field searching.

C. Continuing Research with *One Good Case*

After finding a relevant authority, you can use it as a springboard to find other relevant sources. Suppose you find a helpful case. In LexisNexis, you can immediately Shepardize the case to learn of subsequent cases and secondary authorities that cited it. By restricting the Shepard's search to relevant headnotes, you can narrow your search to those subsequent cases that are most likely to be helpful in your research. Alternatively, clicking on a headnote will lead to a *Search Advisor* screen that allows searching for other cases LexisNexis has indexed under the same topic or headnote. Other LexisNexis options include the *More Like This* or *More Like Selected Text* functions, which ask the computer to find other cases with similar citations or similar language.

The Westlaw equivalent to Shepardizing is to use the KeyCite function, which will list cases and other authorities that cited your case. An additional option on Westlaw is using the topic and key number system, which is discussed in Chapter 6. Review a case on point to identify the topics and key numbers for relevant headnotes. Then use these headnotes as search terms and broaden the list of cases in your results. Clicking on the key number in a case will bring up a screen that prompts a search for additional cases with that key number. Topic-key number searching is often most helpful when combined with search terms.

Note that in both LexisNexis and Westlaw finding *more* cases does not necessarily mean finding absolutely all other relevant cases. It also does not ensure that the cases retrieved will be relevant. You may find many cases that are not applicable and may detract from your research process. You must analyze the cases yourself and determine whether they are relevant.

D. Printing, Downloading, or Emailing Results

Both LexisNexis and Westlaw allow you to download or email documents as opposed to printing them. These options are effective early in your research because they allow you to skim quickly to the point where your terms appear using your computer's *Find* function. Moreover, now that most word processors allow highlighting and in-line

Table 10-4. Example Notes for Online Searching

Date of Search: *November 6, 2008*

Issue: *Whether a covenant not to compete is enforceable in Louisiana*

Online Site or Service: *LexisNexis*

Sources: *Louisiana State Cases (short name: LACTS)*

Search Terms: *covenant, contract, noncompetition, restraint of trade, compete, employee, employer, employment*

Date Restriction: *Last 10 years*

Search: *(covenant or contract) /p (noncompetition or restraint of trade or compete) /p employ!*

Results: *[Either list your results here or print a cite list to attach to your notes.]*

---

annotating, you may choose to read and organize your research documents entirely on your computer. Remember, however, that you must read (and often re-read) relevant documents very carefully, and many researchers still find it easier to do so on paper as opposed to the computer screen.

E. Keeping Track

If you are new to online legal searches, your searches may be more successful if you complete the chart in Table 10-4 before beginning your search. Even after you become experienced in online searching, you should still keep notes containing the dates you searched, the searches you ran, and your results from the searches. These notes will help you stay on track and avoid duplicating research on a later date. Notes will also indicate the time period that needs to be updated as you near your project deadline.

Online services provide lists of past searches and results, and you should form the habit of printing or saving them. On LexisNexis, click *History*. On Westlaw, click *Research Trail*.

F. Research Using WestlawNext, Lexis Advance, and Other Services

As web developers roll out new products to facilitate legal research, their goal is usually to make it easier for the researcher to access the primary and secondary sources discussed throughout this book. The web developers are not creating new sources of law. Thus, researchers using the next generation of any electronic research platform should read or view any tutorials provided by the web developer on how to conduct research using the platform, keeping in mind that what the researcher is looking for, be it primary or secondary sources, remains the same.

For example, WestlawNext and Lexis Advance are the next generation of research platforms developed by West and LexisNexis. They provide a new look and new ways to get to the information gathered by these legal research giants, which is the same information available on their original or classic platforms. Both WestlawNext and Lexis Advance currently allow a researcher to enter a natural language search into a main search box, without first having to select a database or source in which to research. Results are displayed in groups, by the types of sources retrieved with excerpts of the relevant portions of the sources. The researcher can then narrow search results by choosing to just look at one type of source, such as statutes or cases. The researcher can also use post-search filters to narrow results by jurisdiction, date, practice area or topic, among other filters. Additionally, both platforms allow a researcher who has found relevant information in a case to find additional cases on that point of law, using Lexis Advance Legal Issue Trail or West's Key Number System.

The novice researcher must be careful to avoid becoming overwhelmed by the large number of results uncovered through an electronic search. Like the researcher entering a physical law library, the researcher should determine what types of sources will most likely lead to the information sought and consult those sources first. The researcher should also use filters to narrow results, keeping in mind that the goal is rarely to have read everything ever written on a subject in every jurisdiction, but to locate information relevant to the issue on which the researcher is working.

Platforms like WestlawNext and Lexis Advance provide efficient tools for saving and organizing research. Documents can be saved in electronic folders, and the researcher can take notes on documents and highlight relevant passages on the electronic version of the documents. Folders can be shared with others working on the same project. The platforms also keep track of the researcher's prior searches so that research can be done more efficiently with little duplication or backtracking.

Chapter 11

Research Efficiency and Organization

This chapter explains how to develop a strategy for conducting research efficiently and offers suggestions for organizing the documents located through research. It builds on the research advice given throughout the book

Chapter 2 listed six steps to follow to complete a research project from start to finish: (1) perform pre-research tasks, including gathering facts, generating search terms, and formulating a research plan; (2) consult secondary authorities; (3) find controlling constitutional provisions, statutes, or rules; (4) locate and review relevant cases; (5) update legal authorities; and (6) end research when you have no holes in your analysis and when you begin seeing the same authorities repeatedly. This chapter builds on Chapter 2 and the other chapters on specific source research by providing advice on researching efficiently and organizing the information gathered through the research process.

I. Maintaining Your Focus on the Issue

As you research, you will be more effective and efficient if you maintain your focus on the issue you are researching. Sometimes novice researchers, and even some experienced researchers, get sidetracked by interesting cases or discussions of law that are not directly relevant to the issue being researched. Be clear about the issue or issues you are researching and the purpose of your research, and stay focused.

As you begin researching an issue, think broadly about that issue and review general materials, such as secondary sources. However, the sooner you are able to focus your research more particularly on the main issue and on primary sources from your jurisdiction, the better. Of course, on some issues that have not been frequently litigated or discussed, general materials, materials on analogous issues, or materials from other jurisdictions may be the only information available.

II. Keeping Track of What You Find and Choosing What to Keep

A. Keep a Research Log

Keeping track of what you find while researching is necessary for good research, and it also plays a critical role in your writing process. Along with the research plan or strategy, you should keep a *research log* that tracks what you have actually done. This log can be a separate document or it can be added to the research plan, either as a separate section or as a separate column next to the plan that identifies what you have done, what you found, and when. Using the research plan and the research log, you can keep track of sources actually consulted and compare to sources that you planned to consult to ensure that you have thoroughly researched an issue. Often, determining that your research is complete is based on reviewing your process to make sure that you have checked all of the potentially relevant sources.

As you use a source, make notes in your research log that summarize your work in that source. For print research, include the volumes you used, the indexes or tables you reviewed, and the terms you searched for. For computer research, include the site, the specific database or link, and the searches that you entered. List both successful and unsuccessful index terms and searches so that you do not inadvertently repeat these same steps later, or so you can revisit a dead end that later becomes relevant. Note the date that you performed each search.

B. Choose What to Keep

In addition to keeping track of where you have researched, you need to keep track of the information you have reviewed and choose what to keep. Legal researchers frequently fall somewhere on the spectrum between being *the collector* and being *too picky.* The collector copies or prints just about everything she ever touches with little or no discretion as to whether the source is helpful and worth keeping. She has some sense of satisfaction that she has found *something* through her research, but eventually this researcher realizes that she has collected more than she has time to review.

On the other end of the spectrum is the researcher who is too picky. This researcher is looking for a case that has the same facts and issues as the case she is researching. She has little to show for the hours spent researching because no source she has reviewed is just perfect and on point. She is anxious, sure that the source is out there, but that she is missing it.

To some degree, most researchers have felt like these researchers at one time or another. Keep the following tips in mind as you research to maintain some balance between these extremes.

- Before deciding to print or copy a secondary source, like a law review or encyclopedia article, read the introduction for a description of what the article addresses to determine if the source is worth a careful read. ALR annotations even have a description of what is and is not included and cross references to other related annotations. Similarly, read the syllabus and headnotes of cases to determine if the cases address an issue similar to yours. Read constitutional provisions, statutes, rules, and regulations carefully, as well as some of the initial annotations to these sources, if annotated, to determine if the provision is relevant. When reviewing annotations, consider whether the *legally significant facts* of the cases described are similar to the facts of your case. Legally significant facts are facts that are relevant to the analysis of an issue under the law.
- Look for good statements of the law, not only in constitutional and statutory provisions, but also in cases. Courts that clearly

state the law often provide a structure for an analysis under that law. The court might identify elements, requirements, factors, or considerations around which your analysis will be structured. Also, look for cases with analogous facts that you can compare and contrast to your client's facts.

- Be an active writer while you research. Note on the top of the sources you decide to print why you have decided to do so. You might note that a particular case has a good statement of the overall rule and that it would be a good case to compare on element two of that rule. You might note that another source provides a good discussion of the policy behind a rule. These notations will save you time later when you review the sources, organize your work into an outline, and draft your analysis.

- Compile a list of sources on which you record the names and citations of all sources you will review. As you review sources, add to this list any other sources referenced in the sources you review that are worth pursuing. Note on this list when you review a source so that you do not duplicate your efforts.

C. Take Good Notes and Organize

Once you have decided which sources are worth a more careful read, begin to work your way through those sources. Choose an organizational scheme for reading them carefully in groups. For example, if there is a constitutional provision, statute, or rule on point, begin by reading it carefully, then move to reading cases that interpret the provision. One approach is to read cases from the most recently decided to the older cases so that you begin with the most up-to-date and synthesized version of the law.

Take notes on your sources, rather than just highlighting, and be sure to record how a source is helpful and how you plan to use it. Taking notes, rather than simply highlighting, also helps to ensure you understand what you are reading. If you determine that a source is not helpful after a more careful read, write that on the first page of the source as well on your notes and on your source list.

Begin a new page for your notes on each source, whether you are typing those notes on a computer or you are handwriting. The benefit of this practice is that you will be able to work with notes on one source without being distracted by notes on another source. Additionally, you will be able to separate notes by topic or issue more easily.

Record full citation information for sources so that you do not have to go back to re-gather information. This step includes keeping track of exact page numbers for pinpoint citations and using quotation marks around information that is directly quoted. An easy way to keep track of page numbers for pinpoint citation purposes is to set page numbers off in the margin of your notes whenever you change pages.

When taking notes on statutes or similar provisions, write down the exact language of the statute or attach a copy of the statute to your notes. In your notes, break down the statute into its parts. Read the statutes immediately before and after the statute, looking for related provisions, and record any definitions provided. Check for cross references to other statutes, and review annotations. When reviewing annotations, look for references to cases with good statements of the law and look for references to cases with facts similar to your facts. Record the citations to additional sources to review on your list.

When taking notes on cases, brief the cases, but with a focus on the issues relevant to your research. Thus, if a case includes a discussion of an evidentiary issue and a discussion on the court's jurisdiction, and your research focuses only on the evidentiary issue, then just brief that part of the case. Include the relevant facts, the procedural history, the court's holding and reasoning on the relevant issue or issues, and any rules applied by the court. In addition, as noted above, include information on citation, updating, and the case's relevance to your research.

Further, when reading several cases, consider the level of the deciding courts, the dates of the decisions, and how the decisions relate to each other. Also, consider whether any case seems to be the case to which most courts cite on the issue.

Finally, for any source that can be updated, have a system to keep track of what you have updated so that you do not unnecessarily repeat updating and you do not forget to update every primary source. A good practice is to write directly on your notes on the source and on your source list that you have updated a source and when you did so. Printing or saving citation lists is also effective.

III. Updating

Plan to update each source twice: once to ensure that the source is good law and to locate additional authorities that have cited the source, and a second time just before completing your assignment to ensure that sources remain good law. As is mentioned above, be sure to keep track of what you have updated.

IV. Outlining the Analysis

Because the most effective research often occurs in conjunction with the analysis of your particular project, try to develop an outline that addresses your client's problem as soon as you can. If outlining feels too restrictive, you may benefit from a chart that organizes all the primary authority by issue or element, such as in Table 11-1.

Your first analytical outline or chart may be based on information in a secondary source, the requirements of a statute, or the elements of a common law claim. It will become more sophisticated and detailed as you conduct your research. Recognize that you cannot reread every case or statute in its entirety each time you need to include it in your outline; instead, refer to your notes and briefs to find the key ideas supporting each step in your analysis.

The outline or chart should enable you to synthesize the law, apply the law to your client's facts, and reach a conclusion on the desired outcome. Applying the law to your client's facts may lead you to research issues that may not be apparent in a merely theoretical discussion of the law.

Table 11-1. Sample Analysis Chart

Research Question: Is a letter opener considered a *dangerous weapon* such that defendant should be charged with aggravated battery? *Controlling Statutes*: La. Rev. Stat. Ann. §§ 14:2, 14:34.

Issue	Case	Rule	Facts	Holding
1. Is object inherently dangerous?	a. *Bowers*, 909 So. 2d 1038 (La. Ct. App. 2d Cir. 2005).	A gun used in connection with and at the scene of a robbery is, as a matter of law, inherently dangerous.	Defendant pulled gun on victim during the course of the robbery and threatened victim.	Gun was considered inherently dangerous.
	b. *Legendre*, 362 So. 2d 570 (La. 1978).	Some objects are considered dangerous weapons because they are inherently dangerous.	Defendant slammed victim's head into concrete parking lot.	Concrete parking lot is not an inherently dangerous object.
2. How was object used?	a. *Johnson*, 598 So. 2d 1152 (La. Ct. App. 1st Cir. 1992).	An inherently harmless object can be considered a dangerous weapon when its use is likely to cause death or great bodily harm.	Ink pen was used by defendant to facilitate robbery. Defendant stabbed victim with pen.	Ink pen used in robbery was a dangerous weapon because it was used to stab victim and facilitate crime.
	b. *Clark*, 527 So. 2d 542 (La. Ct. App. 3d Cir. 1988).	Even if an inherently harmless object does not actually cause serious bodily harm, it can be considered a dangerous weapon because of the likelihood of resulting serious harm or death under the circumstances.	Defendant threw metal sign post at victim and hit victim with it. Victim was not seriously injured.	Metal sign post was a dangerous weapon even though resulting injuries were not serious.
	c. *McClure*, 793 So. 2d 454 (La. Ct. App. 2d Cir. 2001).	In addition to the character of the weapon, consider by whom, upon whom, and how a weapon is used to assess whether it is calculated to produce great bodily harm.	Defendant used a piece of wood to strike victim in the head, which knocked victim to the ground and caused him serious bodily injury.	Resulting harm from blow by stick that knocked victim to the ground and required that he get sutures supported finding that stick was a dangerous weapon.

V. Ending Research

One of the most difficult problems new researchers face is deciding when to stop researching and begin writing. Often deadlines imposed by the court or a supervisor will limit the amount of time spent on a research project. The expense to the client will also be a consideration.

Sometimes you will find a clear answer and you know your research is over. Even without finding a clear answer, when your research in various sources leads back to the same authorities, you can be confident that you have been thorough. As a final checklist, go through each step of the basic research process to ensure you have considered each one. Review your research plan and research log for this particular project.

If you have worked through the research process and found nothing, it may be that nothing exists. Before reaching that conclusion, expand your research terms and look in a few more secondary sources. Consider whether other jurisdictions may have helpful persuasive authority.

Remember that the goal of legal research is to solve a client's problem. Sometimes the law will not seem to support the solution that your client had in mind. Think creatively to address the client's problem in a different way. While you must tell your supervisor or your client when a desired approach is not feasible, you will want to have prepared an alternate solution if possible.

VI. Presenting Your Findings

Once you have completed your research, document your findings so that you have a record of what you have done and what you have found. You might write a legal memorandum for the file or for another attorney, a letter to a client, a motion and supporting memorandum for the court, a brief, or even a bench memorandum if you are working for a judge. Whatever your audience and whatever is the appropriate document in which to record your work, below are some simple tips to assist in presenting your research and analysis. Consult a legal writing text for a more in-depth discussion of this topic.

A. Determine What Is Expected

Determine what you are expected to produce as a result of your research. While sometimes you may simply be asked to locate the law and provide citations or copies of relevant documents, more often than not you will be expected to provide a written report of your findings. This report may require you to provide an analysis of a legal issue based on your research. Rarely will you be asked to just brief the relevant cases. If you are asked for analysis, predict how the law you have found will or should be applied to your facts and issue.

B. Begin with Mandatory Authority

Present research and analysis beginning with mandatory authority when available. Of mandatory authorities, enacted law should usually precede other sources of mandatory authority. (But see Section VI.C below on moving from general to specific principles.) Supplement mandatory authority with persuasive authority when necessary to explain the law or provide examples of the application of similar law. Additionally, present persuasive authority when mandatory authority does not exist.

C. Move from General to Specific Principles

When explaining the applicable law, move from general to more specific principles. For example, you may present a four-part test first, followed by specific rules or definitions of principles used in the four-part test. Proof of negligence may require proof of a duty, breach, causation, and damages. Set out the four-part test, which is the general rule of negligence, then before analyzing each part of the test, give the rule or definition of what is required for that part to be proven.

D. Use Prior Decisions Properly to Support Analysis

Prior decisions may be used for two purposes in your analysis. First, you may extract or induce a rule from a prior decision. Second, you may use a prior decision to explain or illustrate how a rule has been applied in the past, sometimes referred to as a precedent or analogous case discussion. When relying on a prior decision for a rule, state the rule clearly first without bogging the reader down in the specific facts to which the rule was applied. When a discussion of the facts and the court's analysis is helpful to explain or illustrate the rule, then provide this information, being sure to include the relevant facts, the court's reasoning, and the court's holding.

E. Be a Skeptic

Be skeptical and question your analysis and conclusions. Anticipate and address potential counter arguments or weaknesses. You will strengthen your analysis by considering what you or someone else might argue to support a view that runs counter to your conclusions. When appropriate, raise these counter arguments and rebut them.

Appendix A

Legal Citation

A legal document must convince a lawyer or a judge reading it that its arguments were well researched and its analysis is well supported. One way legal writers do this is by providing references to the authorities used to develop that analysis and reach the conclusion. These references are called *legal citations.* They tell the reader where to find the authorities relied on and indicate the level of analytical support the authorities provide.[1] See Table A-1. In a legal document, every legal rule and every explanation of the law must be cited. All quotations must be attributed to their source, as well, showing what language is being quoted exactly.

Legal citations are included in the text of legal documents rather than being saved for a bibliography. While law students initially feel that these citations clutter documents, attorneys appreciate the valuable information that citations provide.

The format used to convey citation information requires meticulous attention to such riveting details as whether a space is needed between two abbreviations. In this respect, citation format rules can be like fundamental writing rules, which are based on convention, not reason. Why capitalize the personal pronoun *I* but not *we* or *you* or *they*? Why does a comma signify a pause, while a period indicates a stop? Rather than trying to understand why citations are formatted the way they are, the most practical approach is simply to learn cita-

---

1. ALWD & Darby Dickerson, *ALWD Citation Manual* 3 (4th ed. 2010); *The Bluebook: A Uniform System of Citation* 1 (Columbia Law Review Ass'n et al. eds., 19th ed. 2010).

Table A-1. Purposes of Legal Citation

- Show the reader where to find the cited material in the original case, statute, rule, article, or other authority.

- Indicate the weight and persuasiveness of each authority, for example, by specifying the court that decided the case, the author of a document, and the publication date of the authority.

- Convey the type and degree of support the authority offers, for example, by indicating whether the authority supports your point directly or only implicitly.

- Demonstrate that the analysis in your document is the result of careful research.

Source: *ALWD Citation Manual.*

tion rules and apply them. Frequent repetition will make them second nature.

Use of proper citation form also signals to the reader that the writer pays attention to details, an important quality for a legal researcher and writer to have. A reader who has confidence in the writer is more likely to trust the research and analysis being conveyed through the writing.

Of the many different citation systems that exist, this chapter addresses Louisiana citation rules and custom, as well as the two national citation manuals, the *ALWD Citation Manual: A Professional System of Citation* and *The Bluebook: A Uniform System of Citation.* In law practice, you may encounter state statutes, court rules, and style manuals that dictate the form of citation used before the courts of different states. You may find that each firm or agency that you work for has its own preference for citation or makes minor variations to generally accepted format. Some law offices have their own style manuals, drawn from state rules and national manuals. Once you are aware of the basic function and format of citation, adapting to a slightly different set of rules is not difficult.

I. Louisiana Citation Rules

Most states have their own rules of citation, called *local court citation rules*. These rules may differ somewhat from the rules of other states and the rules in the two national citation manuals. In Louisiana, custom dictates many citation rules. Custom has been influenced by suggested citation forms from West, which has published the official reporter and the official version of Louisiana statutes and rules for many years.

Additionally, the courts have promulgated a couple of citation rules regarding case citations: Louisiana Supreme Court General Administrative Rules part G, rule 8 and Louisiana Uniform Rules of the Courts of Appeal 2-14.2. Citations to cases in documents filed in the Louisiana Courts of Appeal and the Louisiana Supreme Court are to conform to rule 8, and rule 2-14.2 applies to citations in documents filed with the Louisiana Courts of Appeal. Lawyers practicing in Louisiana often omit the public domain citation information required by the Supreme Court rule, though this practice is changing. The rule went into effect on July 2, 1994. See Tables A-2 and A-3 for the complete text of these court rules.

One of the biggest differences between the national citation manuals and local practice in Louisiana is the way sources are abbreviated. Table A-4 shows the comparisons of citation forms for Louisiana primary sources. Many years ago, West recommended abbreviations for Louisiana enacted law, which are used by many Louisiana judges and practitioners. Additionally, the Supreme Court rule and many Louisiana judges and practitioners omit a space between the *So.* and the *2d* when they abbreviate this reporter. The other primary difference is the way that Louisiana Courts of Appeal are designated. The most widely used designation is *La. App.* followed by either *1 Cir.* or *1st Cir.*

An additional resource on citing to Louisiana and French sources is M.A. Cunningham, *Guide to Louisiana and Selected French Legal Materials and Citations*, 67 Tul. L. Rev. 1305 (1993), which is especially helpful to the researcher who must cite to older sources.

Table A-2. Louisiana Supreme Court General Administrative Rules pt. G, r. 8

A. The following rules of citation of Louisiana appellate court decisions shall apply:

(1) Opinions and actions issued by the Supreme Court of Louisiana and the Louisiana Courts of Appeal following December 31, 1993 shall be cited according to a uniform public domain citation form with a parallel citation to West's Southern Reporter:

(a) The uniform public domain citation form shall consist of the case name, docket number excluding letters, court abbreviation, and month, day and year of issue, and be followed by a parallel citation to West's Southern Reporter, e.g.:

Smith v. Jones, 93-2345 (La. 7/15/94); 650 So.2d 500, or *Smith v. Jones*, 93-2345 (La. App. 1 Cir. 7/15/94); 660 So.2d 400

(b) If a pinpoint public domain citation is needed, the page number designated by the court shall follow the docket number and be set off with a comma and the abbreviation "p.", and may be followed by a parallel pinpoint citation to West's Southern Reporter, e.g.:

Smith v. Jones, 94-2345, p. 7 (La. 7/15/94); 650 So.2d 500, 504

(2) Opinions issued by the Supreme Court of Louisiana for the period between December 31, 1972 and January 1, 1994, and all opinions issued by the Courts of Appeal from the beginning of their inclusion in West's Southern Reporter in 1928 until January 1, 1994, shall be cited according to the form in West's Southern Reporter:

(a) The citation will consist of the case name, Southern Reporter volume number, title abbreviation, page number, court designation, and year, e.g.:

Smith v. Jones, 645 So.2d 321 (La. 1990)

(b) A parallel public domain citation following the same format as that for post-January 1, 1994 opinions may be added after the Southern Reporter citation, but is not required.

(3) Opinions issued by the Supreme Court of Louisiana prior to the discontinuation of the official Louisiana Reports in 1972 and opinions issued by the Courts of Appeal prior to their inclusion in the Southern Reporter in 1928 shall be cited in accordance with pre-1994 practice, as follows:

Table A-2. Louisiana Supreme Court General Administrative Rules pt. G, r. 8, *continued*

(a) Cite to Louisiana Reports, Louisiana Annual Reports, Robinson, Martin, Reports of the Louisiana Courts of Appeal, Peltier, Teisser, or McGloin if therein, and to the Southern Reporter or Southern 2d if therein.

(b) A parallel public domain citation following the same format as that for post-January 1, 1994 opinions may be added, but is not required.

B. These rules shall apply to all published actions of the Supreme Court of Louisiana and the Louisiana Courts of Appeal issued after December 31, 1993. Citation under these rules in court documents shall become mandatory for all documents filed after July 1, 1994.

Table A-3. Louisiana Uniform Rules of the Court of Appeal 2-12.4

Citation of Louisiana cases shall be in conformity with Section VIII of the Louisiana Supreme Court General Administrative Rules. Citations of other cases shall be to volume and page of the official reports (and when possible to the unofficial reports). It is recommended that where United States Supreme Court cases are cited, all three reports be cited, e.g., *Miranda v. Arizona*, 384 U.S. 436, 86 S.Ct. 1602, 16 L.Ed.2d 694 (1966). When a decision from another state is cited, a copy thereof should be attached to the brief.

II. Other States' Citation Rules

When working in another state, follow that state's local rules or use the format given in the *ALWD Citation Manual* or *The Bluebook*, depending on your supervisor's preferences. Appendix 2 of the *ALWD Citation Manual* identifies local court citation rules for all states. Similarly, Table 2 of the Bluepages in *The Bluebook* refers to citation rules for specific jurisdictions. Like Louisiana, many states have citation rules promulgated by courts.

Table A-4. Comparisons of Citation Formats for Louisiana Citations

Publication/ Deciding Court for Cases	Customary or Acceptable Practice in Louisiana	*ALWD Citation Manual*	*The Bluebook*
Louisiana Constitution of 1974	La. Const. art. x, §x.	La. Const. art. x, §x.	La. Const. art. x, §x.
West's Louisiana Statutes Annotated— Louisiana Civil Code	LSA–C.C. art. xxx (year), La. Civ. Code art. xxx (year), or *ALWD* and *Bluebook* form.	La. Civ. Code Ann. art. xxx (year).	La. Civ. Code Ann. art. xxx (year).
—Louisiana Revised Statutes	LSA–R.S. x:xxx (year), La.R.S. x:xxx (year), or *Bluebook* form.	La. Rev. Stat. Ann. §x:xxx (year).	La. Rev. Stat. Ann. §x:xxx (year).
—Louisiana Code of Civil Procedure	LSA–C.C.P. art. xx (year), La. Code Civ. Proc. art. xx (year), or *Bluebook* form.	La. Code Civ. Proc. Ann. art. xx (year).	La. Code Civ. Proc. Ann. art. xx (year).
—Louisiana Code of Criminal Procedure	LSA–C.Cr.P. art. xx (year), La. Code Crim. Proc. art. xx (year), or *Bluebook* form.	La. Code Crim. Proc. Ann. art. xx (year).	La. Code Crim. Proc. Ann. art. xx (year).
—Louisiana Code of Evidence	LSA–C.E. art. xx (year), La. Code Evid. art. xx (year), or *Bluebook* form.	La Code Evid. Ann. art. xx (year).	La. Code Evid. Ann. art. xx (year).
—Louisiana Children's Code	LSA–Ch.C. art. xx (year), La. Child. Code art. xx (year), or *Bluebook* form.	La. Child. Code Ann. art. xx (year).	La. Child. Code Ann. art. xx (year).
Louisiana Administrative Code	LAC title#:section# (year) or *ALWD* and *Bluebook* form.	La. Admin. Code tit. x, §x (year).	La. Admin. Code tit. x, §x (year).

Table A-4. Comparisons of Citation Formats for
Louisiana Citations, *continued*

Publication/ Deciding Court for Cases	Customary or Acceptable Practice in Louisiana	*ALWD Citation Manual*	*The Bluebook*
Southern Reporter and *Southern Reporter, Second* —Louisiana Supreme Court	*Smith v. Jones*, 93-2345 (La. 7/15/94); 650 So.2d 500 or *ALWD* and *Bluebook* form. (A comma is sometimes substituted for the semicolon.)	*Smith v. Jones*, 650 So. 2d 500 (La. 1994).	*Smith v. Jones*, 650 So. 2d 500 (La. 1994).
—Louisiana Court of Appeal	*Smith v. Jones*, 93-2345 (La. App. 1 Cir. 7/15/94); 660 So.2d 400 or *ALWD* form. (A comma is sometimes substituted for the semicolon.)	*Smith v. Jones*, 660 So. 2d 400 (La. App. 1st Cir. 1994).	*Smith v. Jones*, 660 So. 2d 400 (La. Ct. App. 1994) or (La. Ct. App. 1st 1994).

III. The National Citation Manuals

While state citation rules often provide just rules and examples, national citation manuals also attempt to explain the components of citations. Student editors of four law reviews have developed citation rules that are published as *The Bluebook: A Uniform System of Citation*, now in its nineteenth edition. An author submitting an article for publication in one of those law reviews, or in other law reviews that adhere to *The Bluebook* rules, should follow *The Bluebook* citation format.

Until the *ALWD Citation Manual* was first published in 2000, *The Bluebook* was the only national citation system that was widely recognized. Many law firms, agencies, and organizations still consider *Bluebook* citations the norm, although few practicing lawyers know its current rules; most assume that *Bluebook* rules have not changed since they were in law school. Many lawyers refer to checking citations as *Bluebooking.*

For practicing lawyers, the primary difficulty with *The Bluebook* is that it includes *two* citation systems: one for law review articles and another for legal memoranda and court documents. Most of *The Bluebook*'s over 400 pages are devoted to citations used for articles published in law journals. The rules most important to lawyers, those concerning legal memoranda and court documents, are given less attention in *The Bluebook*.

When using *The Bluebook* for citations in legal memoranda and court documents, a student or lawyer using *The Bluebook* must use the *Bluepages*, a section near the front of *The Bluebook*, to translate each example into the format used in legal documents in practice. (Previous editions contained a much shorter section called *Practitioner's Notes*.) Another helpful feature is the reference guide on the inside back cover of the book, which gives examples of citations used in court documents and legal memoranda.[2]

One of the biggest differences in form between *The Bluebook* for law review articles and its Bluepages for practitioners is the font used. *The Bluebook* uses a different type — LARGE AND SMALL CAPITAL LETTERS — for law review citations for such things as statutory and law review publications. The Bluepages and the *ALWD Citation Manual* employ only ordinary type and *italics* or <u>underlining</u>. The Bluepages list items that should be italicized or underlined in citations in legal memoranda and court documents. These include case names, titles of books and articles, and introductory signals. Items not included in the list should appear in ordinary type. Remember to follow the instructions in this list even when *The Bluebook* examples include large and small capital letters.

The *ALWD Citation Manual* may be the best manual for novices because it uses a single system of citation for legal memoranda, court documents, law review articles, and all other legal documents. The explanations are clear, and the examples are useful to law students, practicing lawyers, and other legal professionals.

Regardless of which citation manual you use, the key to mastering proper citation is actually looking up the proper citation form in the

---

2. Examples of law review citations are found on the inside front cover.

Table A-5. Examples of Citation Sentences and Citation Clauses

---

Citation Sentences: Simple burglary of an inhabited dwelling includes burglary of structures used as places of abode, such as houses and apartments. La. Rev. Stat. Ann. § 14:62.2 (2007). A person need not be present in the dwelling at the moment of the burglary as long as it is proven that a person was living in the dwelling at the time. *State v. Tran*, 709 So. 2d 311, 317 (La. Ct. App. 5th Cir. 1998).

Citation Clauses: Louisiana law defines both simple burglary of an inhabited dwelling, La Rev. Stat. Ann. § 14:62.2 (2007), and unauthorized entry of an inhabited dwelling, *id.* § 14:62.3, which are related, but different, offenses.

---

manual. Both manuals have numerous rules that are well indexed. With every citation question you encounter, assume that the manual has a rule and consult the index to find it.

A. Incorporating Citations into a Document

A legal document must provide a citation for each idea that comes from a case, statute, article, or other source. Thus, paragraphs that state legal rules and explain the law should contain many citations. *ALWD* Rule 43.2; *Bluebook* Rule B1.[3]

A citation may offer support for an entire sentence or for an idea expressed in part of a sentence. If the citation supports the entire sentence, it is placed in a separate *citation sentence* that begins with a capital letter and ends with a period. *ALWD* Rule 43.1(a); *Bluebook* Rule B2. If the citation supports only a portion of the sentence, it is included immediately after the relevant part of that sentence and set off from the sentence by commas in what is called a *citation clause*. *ALWD* Rule 43.1(b); *Bluebook* Rule B2. Table A-5 provides examples of each.

---

3. Throughout this chapter, references will be provided to *ALWD* and *Bluebook* rule numbers in this fashion: manual and rule. References to *The Bluebook* that begin with *B* are to sections in the Bluepages.

You should not cite a client's facts or your conclusions about a case, statute, or other authority. The following sentence should not be cited: "Under the facts presented, Mr. Client's conduct would fall under first-degree burglary because a homeless family sometimes slept in the building he broke into." These facts and conclusions are unique to your situation and would not be found anywhere in the reference source.

B. Case Citations

A full citation to a case includes (1) the name of the case, (2) the volume and reporter in which the case is published, (3) the first page of the case, (4) the exact page in the case that contains the idea you are citing (*i.e.,* the *pinpoint* or *jump* cite), (5) the court that decided the case, and (6) the date the case was decided. *ALWD* Rule 12; *Bluebook* Rules B5 and 10. The key points in these rules for citation to cases are given below, along with examples.

1. Essential Components of Case Citations

Include the name of just the first party on each side, even if several are listed in the case caption. Do not designate additional parties with *et al.* If the party is an individual, include only the party's last name. If the party is a business or organization, shorten the party's name by using the abbreviations in *ALWD* Appendix 3 or *Bluebook* Table 6.

Although many of the abbreviations are the same in both citation manuals, one variation concerns the use of apostrophes in abbreviations. *The Bluebook* abbreviates some words with periods and others with apostrophes. The *ALWD Citation Manual* uses only periods. See Table A-6 for some abbreviation comparisons. Additionally, under *Bluebook* rules, *United States* is never abbreviated when it is a party's name, *Bluebook* Rules B5.1.1 and 10.2.2, but it is abbreviated according to *ALWD* Rule 12.2(g).

Recent editions of *The Bluebook* have changed the rule concerning the abbreviation of the first word of a party's name. Under earlier edi-

Table A-6. Comparison of Select Word Abbreviations
in *ALWD* and *The Bluebook*

	ALWD Manual	*The Bluebook*
Word	(Appendix 3)	(Table T6)
Associate	Assoc.	Assoc.
Association	Assn. or Ass'n	Ass'n
Center	Ctr.	Ctr.
Commissioner	Commr. or Comm'r	Comm'r
Department	Dept. or Dep't	Dep't
Hospital	Hosp.	Hosp.

tions, the first word of a party's name could never be abbreviated, unless the name was a common abbreviation like NAACP, the National Association for the Advancement of Colored People. In the current edition, each word in a party's name that appears in Table T6 is abbreviated in citations, even if it is the first word.

Between the parties' names, place a lower case "v" followed by a period. Do not use a capital "V" or the abbreviation "vs." Place a comma after the second party's name; do not italicize or underline this comma.

The parties' names may be italicized or underlined. Use the style preferred by your supervisor, and use that style consistently throughout each document. Do not combine italics and underlining in one cite or within a single document.

Example: *Harris v. Fla. Elections Commn.*, 235 F.3d 578,
580 (11th Cir. 2000).

Next, give the volume and the reporter in which the case is found. Pay special attention to whether the reporter is in its first, second, or third series. Abbreviations for reporters are found in *ALWD* Appendix 1 and *Bluebook* Table T1, which are organized by jurisdiction. In *ALWD*, state information precedes the federal citation information, and in *The Bluebook* the federal citation information precedes state information. In the example above, 235 is the volume number and F.3d is the reporter abbreviation for *Federal Reporter, Third Series.*

After the reporter name, include both the first page of the case and the pinpoint page containing the idea that you are referencing, separated by a comma and a space. *ALWD* Rules 5 and 12.5; *Bluebook* B5.1.2. The first page of the *Harris* case above is 578, and the page containing the specific idea being cited is 580. If the pinpoint page you are citing is also the first page of the case, then the same page number will appear twice even though this seems repetitive.[4]

In a parenthetical following this information, indicate the court that decided the case. Court abbreviations are included in *ALWD* Appendices 1 and 4, and *Bluebook* Tables T1 and T7. See also *ALWD* Rule 12.6(a), and *Bluebook* Rule B5.1.3. In the above example, the Eleventh Circuit Court of Appeals, a federal court, decided the case.

If the reporter abbreviation clearly indicates which court decided a case, do not repeat this information in the parenthetical. Only cases of the United States Supreme Court are reported in *United States Reports*, abbreviated U.S., so you need not include a court designation in a citation to that reporter. Similarly, *Louisiana Reports*, abbreviated La., was the official reporter for Louisiana Supreme Court decisions prior to 1972; this reporter only reported Louisiana Supreme Court decisions. Repeating court abbreviations in citations to these reporters would be duplicative. By contrast, *Southern Reporter, Second Series*, abbreviated So. 2d, publishes decisions from different courts within several states, so the court that decided a particular case needs to be indicated parenthetically. Thus, in the last example below, *Ala.* indicates that the decision came from the Alabama Supreme Court rather than from another court whose decisions are also published in this reporter.

Examples: *Brown v. Bd. of Educ.*, 349 U.S. 294, 300 (1955).

Pelican State Assocs., Inc. v. Winder, 253 La. 697, 700 (1969).

---

4. When using an online version of a case, remember that a reference to a specific reporter page may change in the middle of a computer screen or a printed page. This means that the page number indicated at the top of the screen or printed page may not be the page where the relevant information is located. For example, if the notation *581 appeared in the text before the relevant information, the pinpoint cite would be to page 581, not page 580.

Acceptance Ins. Co. v. Brown, 832 So. 2d 1, 12 (Ala. 2001).

Note that these court abbreviations are not the same as postal codes. Abbreviating the Alabama Supreme Court as AL would be incorrect.

The final piece of required information in most cites is the date the case was decided. For cases published in reporters, give only the year of decision, not the month or date. Do not confuse the date of decision with the date on which the case was argued or submitted, the date on which a motion for rehearing was denied, or the publication date of the reporter. *ALWD* Rule 12.7; *Bluebook* Rule 10.5. For citations to cases available only electronically, give the month abbreviation, date, and year. *ALWD* Rule 12.7(c), 12.12(a); *Bluebook* Rules B5.1.3 and 18.1.1. For public domain citations, consult the state rule for the proper way to indicate the date.

2. Full and Short Citations to Cases

The first time you mention a case by name, immediately give its full citation, including all of the information outlined above. *ALWD* Rule 11.1(c); *Bluebook* Rules B5.2 and B5.3. Even though it is technically correct to include the full citation at the beginning of a sentence, a full citation takes up considerable space and can distract the reader from your point. To focus the reader on the information you are conveying, revise the sentence by moving the case reference and citation to the end of the sentence. Use the premier position in the sentence for your most important information. The simple revision in Table A-7 demonstrates how to avoid the interrupting citation and strengthen the point you are making.

After a full citation has been used once to introduce an authority, short citations are subsequently used to cite to this same authority. A short citation provides just enough information to allow the reader to locate the longer citation and find the pinpoint page. *ALWD* Rules 11.2 and 11.3; *Bluebook* B5.2 and Rules 4 and 10.9.

Use *id.* as the short cite when (1) the cite is to the immediately preceding authority, and (2) the immediately preceding authority contains only one citation, excluding parentheticals that may include ci-

Table A-7. Examples of Full Citations

Assume that this is the first time the case has been mentioned in this document.

CORRECT: (but should be avoided)	In *Day v. City of Fontana*, 19 P.3d 1196, 1198 (Cal. 2001), the court noted that the intent of the legislature that enacted a statute needs to be determined.
REVISION:	The court must determine the intent of the legislature that enacted a statute. *Day v. City of Fontana*, 19 P.3d 1196, 1198 (Cal. 2001).

---

tations. When the second cite is to a different page within the same source, follow the *id.* with "at" and the new pinpoint page number. Capitalize *id.* when it begins a citation sentence, just as the beginning of any sentence is capitalized. *ALWD* Rule 11.3(d); *Bluebook* B5.2.

If the cite is from a source that is not the immediately preceding cite, give the name of one of the parties (generally the first party named in the full cite), the volume, the reporter, and the pinpoint page following "at." *ALWD* Rule 11.2 and Rule 12.21(b); *Bluebook* B5.2.

> Example: Open and notorious possession requires that the claimants prove that the owners had notice that the claimants were asserting title to the disputed property. *Slak v. Porter*, 128 Or. App. 274, 278 (1994). The notice may be actual or constructive. *Id.* at 279. Owners have actual notice when they are aware that their claim of the land is being challenged. *See id.* Constructive notice is satisfied when claimants use the property in a manner considered to give the owner knowledge of their use and claim. *Hoffman v. Freeman Land & Timber, LLC*, 329 Or. 554, 559 (1999). Construction of a fence is recognized as the classic example of open and notorious possession. *Slak*, 128 Or. App. at 279.

If you refer to the case by name in the sentence, your short citation does not need to repeat the case name, *ALWD* Rule 12.21(c), though lawyers often do. The last sentence of the example would also be correct as follows: "In *Slak*, construction of a fence was recognized as the classic example of open and notorious possession. 128 Or. App. at 279."

The format, *Slak* at 279, consisting of just a case name and page number, is incorrect. The volume and reporter abbreviation are also needed.

3. Prior and Subsequent History

Sometimes a citation needs to show what happened to a case at an earlier or later stage of litigation. The case you are citing may have reversed an earlier case, as in the example below. If you are citing a case for a court's analysis of one issue and a later court reversed only on the second issue, you need to alert your reader to that reversal. Or, if you decide for historical purposes to include a discussion of a case that was later overruled, your reader needs to know that as soon as you introduce the case. Prior and subsequent history can be appended to the full citations discussed above. *ALWD* Rules 12.8–12.10; *Bluebook* B5.1.5 and Rule 10.7.

Example: The only time that the Supreme Court addressed the requirement of motive for an EMTALA claim, the court rejected that requirement. *Roberts v. Galen of Va.*, 525 U.S. 249, 253 (1999), *rev'g* 111 F.3d 405 (6th Cir. 1997).

C. Federal Statutory Citations

The general rule for citing federal laws is to cite the *United States Code* (U.S.C.), which is the official code for federal statutes. In reality, that publication is published so slowly that the current language will most likely be found in a commercial code, either *United States Code Annotated* (published by West) or *United States Code Service* (published by LexisNexis). A cite to a federal statute includes the title number, code name, section, publisher (except for U.S.C.), and date. *ALWD* Rule 14.2; *Bluebook* Rule B6.1.1.

The date given in statutory cites is the date of the volume in which the statute is published, not the date the statute was enacted. Think of the date as an address. You are sending your reader to the book in which he can find the text of the statute to which you are citing. You are not trying to send your reader to an old version of the statute, nor are you trying to send your reader to the Notes of Decisions or other annotations that follow a statute. Thus, if the language of a portion of the statute is reprinted in the pocket part, include the dates of both the bound volume and the pocket part. If the language appears only in the pocket part, include only the date of the pocket part. *ALWD* Rules 8 and 14.2(f); *Bluebook* Rule 12.3.2.

> Example: (Statutory language appears in both the
>   bound volume and the supplement):
>   28 U.S.C.A. § 1453 (West 2006 & Supp. 2012).

> Example: (Statutory language appears in just the supplement):
>   28 U.S.C.A. § 1453(d) (West Supp. 2012).

D. Signals

A citation must show the level of support each authority provides. You do this by deciding whether to use an introductory signal and, if so, which one. The more common signals are explained in Table A-8 of this chapter. *ALWD* Rule 44; *Bluebook* Rules B4 and 1.2.

E. Explanatory Parentheticals

At the end of a cite, you can append additional information about the authority in parentheses. Sometimes this parenthetical information conveys to the reader the weight of the authority. For example, a case may have been decided *en banc* or *per curiam*. Or the case may have been decided by a narrow split among the judges who heard the case. Parenthetical information also allows you to name the judges who joined in a dissenting, concurring, or plurality opinion. *ALWD* Rule 12.11(a)-(b); *Bluebook* Rules B5.1.4 and 10.6.1.

Table A-8. Common Signals

No signal	• The source cited provides direct support for the idea in the sentence. • The cite identifies the source of a quotation.
See	• The source cited offers implicit support for the idea in the sentence. • The source cited offers support in dicta.
See also	• The source cited provides additional support for the idea in the sentence. • The support offered by *see also* is not as strong or direct as authorities preceded by no signal or by the signal *see*.
E.g.	• Many authorities state the idea in the sentence, and you are citing only one as an example; this signal allows you to cite just one source while letting the reader know that many other sources say the same thing.

An explanatory parenthetical following a signal can convey helpful, additional information in a compressed space. When using this type of parenthetical, be sure that you do not inadvertently hide a critical part of the court's analysis at the end of a long citation, where a reader is likely to skip over it. *ALWD* Rules 12.11(c) and Rule 46; *Bluebook* Rules B11 and 1.5 and 10.6.

> Example: Excluding relevant evidence during a sentencing hearing may deny the criminal defendant due process. *Green v. Georgia*, 442 U.S. 95, 97 (1979) (per curiam) (regarding testimony of co-defendant's confession in rape and murder case).

F. Quotations

Quotations should be used only when the reader needs to see the text exactly as it appears in the original authority. For example, quoting the controlling statutory language can be extremely helpful. As another example, if a well known case explains an analytical point in a particularly insightful way, a quotation may be warranted.

Excessive quotation has three drawbacks. First, quotations interrupt the flow of your writing when the style of the quoted language differs from your own. Second, excessive use of quotations may suggest to the reader that you do not fully comprehend the material; it is much easier to cut and paste together a document from pieces of various cases than to synthesize and explain a rule of law. Quotations should not be used simply because you cannot think of another way to express an idea. Third, unless the reader is interested in the exact language of the source being quoted, readers tend to skip over long quotations, hoping that the writer has explained or summarized the quoted language.

When a quotation is needed, the words, punctuation, and capitalization within the quotation marks must appear *exactly* as they are in the original. Treat a quotation as a photocopy of the original text. Any alterations or omissions must be indicated. Include commas and periods inside quotation marks; place other punctuation outside the quotation marks unless it is included in the original text. Also, try to provide smooth transitions between your text and the quoted text.

For quotations of fifty or more words, set off the quotation in a block that is indented one tab from both the left and the right margins. Single space the quoted material and do not use quotation marks. If you are following the *ALWD Citation Manual*, you should also set off a quotation in this way if the material exceeds four lines of typed text. Following the block quote, double space and return to the left margin to place the citation to the source of the quotation. *ALWD* Rules 47–49; *Bluebook* Rules B12 and 5.

G. Noteworthy Details

The following citation details are second nature to careful and conscientious lawyers, though they frequently trip up novices.

- Use proper ordinal abbreviations. The most confusing are 2d for *Second* and 3d for *Third* because they differ from the standard format. *ALWD* Rule 4.3; *Bluebook* Rule 6.2(b).

- Do not insert a space between abbreviations of single capital letters. For example, there is no space in U.S. Ordinal numbers like 1st, 2d, and 3d are considered single capital letters for purposes of this rule. Thus, there is no space in P.2d or F.3d because 2d and 3d are considered single capital letters. Leave one space between elements of an abbreviation that are not single capital letters. For example, F. Supp. 2d has a space on each side of "Supp." It would be incorrect to write F.Supp.2d. *ALWD* Rule 2.2; *Bluebook* Rule 6.1. But see Section 1 of this chapter, which notes that in Louisiana both So. 2d and So.2d are frequently used.

- In citation sentences, abbreviate case names, court names, months, and reporter names. Do not abbreviate these words when they are part of textual sentences; instead, spell them out as in the example below. *ALWD* Rules 2.1 and 2.3, Appendix 3 (months, case names), Appendix 4 (court names), Appendix 1 (reporters); *Bluebook* Rules B5.3 and 10.2.1, Table T6 (case names), Table T7 (court names), Table T12 (months), and Table T1 (reporters).

Example: The Fifth Circuit explained that it was required under the Seventh Amendment to try to reconcile potentially inconsistent answers on a special verdict form. *Rogers v. McDorman,* 521 F.3d 381, 396 (5th Cir. 2008).

- In legal documents, spell out numbers zero through ninety-nine and use numerals for larger numbers. However, always spell out a number that is the first word of a sentence. *ALWD* Rule 4.2; *Bluebook* Rule 6.2(a). (See these rules for some exceptions.)

H. *The Bluebook*: Citations for Law Review Articles

Using *The Bluebook* to write citations for law review articles is considerably easier than using it for practice documents. As noted above, almost all of the examples given in *The Bluebook* are in law review format. Table A-9 of this chapter summarizes the typeface used for several common sources and gives examples.

Law review articles place citations in footnotes or endnotes, instead of placing citations in the main text of the document. *Bluebook* Rule 1.1(a). Most law review footnotes include text in ordinary type, in italics, and in large and small capital letters. *Bluebook* Rule 2.2(a). This convention is not universal, and each law review selects the typefaces it will use. Some law reviews may use only ordinary type and italics. Others may use just ordinary type. *Bluebook* Rule 2.1.

The typeface used for a case name depends on (1) whether the case appears in the main text of the article or in a footnote and (2) how the case is used. When a case name appears in the main text of the article

Table A-9. *Bluebook* Typeface for Law Review Footnotes

Item	Typeface Used	Example
Cases	Use ordinary type for case names in full citations. (See text for further explanation.)	Legal Servs. Corp. v. Velazquez, 531 U.S. 533 (2001).
Books	Use large and small capital letters for the author and the title.	David S. Romantz & Kathleen Elliott Vinson, Legal Analysis: The Fundamental Skill (2d ed. 2009).
Periodical articles	Use ordinary type for the author's name, italics for the title, and large and small capitals for the periodical.	Adell Louise Amos, *The Use of State Instream Flow Laws for Federal Land: Respecting State Control While Meeting Federal Purposes*, 36 Envir. Law 1237 (2006).
Explanatory phrases	Use italics for all explanatory phrases, such as *aff'g*, *cert. denied*, *rev'd*, and *overruled by*.	Legal Servs. Corp. v. Velazquez, 531 U.S. 533 (2001), *aff'g* 164 F.3d 757 (2d Cir. 1999).
Introductory signals	Use italics for all introductory signals, such as *see* and *e.g.* when they appear in citations, as opposed to text.	*See id.*

or in a textual sentence of a footnote, it is italicized. By contrast, if a footnote contains an embedded citation, the case name is written in ordinary type. Similarly, when a full cite is given in a footnote, the case name is written in ordinary type. But when a short cite is used in footnotes, the case name is italicized. Assuming you are submitting an article to a law review that uses all three typefaces, *Bluebook* Rule 2 dictates which typeface to use for each type of authority.

Law review footnotes use short cites that are generally the same as those used in other documents. The short cite *id.* may be used only if repeating the immediately preceding footnote's authority, and that footnote contains only one authority. *Bluebook* Rule 4.1. One unique *Bluebook* requirement is the "rule of five." This rule states that a short cite may only be used if the source is "*readily found in one of the preceding five footnotes.*" *Bluebook* Rule 10.9 (cases) (emphasis in original); *Bluebook* Rule 12.9 (statutes).

IV. Editing Citations

To be sure that the citations in a document correctly reflect your research and support your analysis, include enough time in the writing and editing process to check citation accuracy. While writing the document, refer frequently to the local rules or to the citation guide required by your supervisor. After you have completely finished writing the text of the document, check the citations carefully again. Be sure that each citation is still accurate after all the revisions you have made. For example, moving a sentence might require you to change an *id.* to another form of short cite, or vice versa. In fact, some careful writers do not insert *id.* citations until they are completely finished writing and revising.

Sometimes editing for citations can take as long as editing for writing mechanics. The time invested in citations is well spent if it enables the person reading your document to quickly find the authorities you cite and to understand your analysis.

Appendix B

Websites of Interest

The websites noted below are particularly helpful to legal researchers because of the material covered, because they are user-friendly, because they include extensive links to other helpful sites, or all of the above. Most of these websites are referenced in earlier chapters of this book when they are helpful for conducting legal research. *Featured information* noted below is meant to provide a sampling of what is found on these websites and is not meant to identify everything available. While this list is not all-inclusive, it identifies some of the most helpful online resources available to the researcher.

I. Websites Focusing on Louisiana Law

Louisiana Supreme Court, www.lasc.org

Featured Information: in-depth information of the Louisiana court system; maps of judicial districts and circuits; all state courts' rules; Louisiana Code of Judicial Conduct; Louisiana Rules of Professional Conduct; supreme court docket and filing information; links to and contact information for Louisiana state, parish, and city courts; searchable database of supreme court opinions from 1996 to the present; forms for court documents; link to search the Law Library of Louisiana catalog; information and links regarding the Louisiana state bar exam, the Louisiana Attorney Disciplinary Committee, and Louisiana continuing legal education (CLE) requirements.

Notably, because this website provides links to state, parish, and city court websites, those websites are not provided or discussed below. Individual court websites often provide vital information to lawyers who have business in the court, such as access to online court records, extensive court forms, docket information, scheduling information, and contact and filing information. Additionally, many of these websites include their own sets of helpful links to local, parish, state, and federal government and non-government entities.

Louisiana State Legislature, www.legis.state.la.us

Featured Information: in-depth information on the Louisiana legislature; brief descriptions of the Louisiana Civil Code, Revised Statutes, Code of Civil Procedure, Code of Criminal Procedure, Code of Evidence, Children's Code, Louisiana Constitution, Constitution Ancillaries, House Rules, Senate Rules, and Joint Rules; search engine that allows searching of unannotated versions of the laws and rules listed above; search engine that allows bill tracking and legislative history research; links to the *Louisiana Administrative Code*, the *Louisiana Register*, the Public Service Commission Rules, the Civil Service Rules, Attorney General's Opinions, Campaign Finance Opinions, Ethics Opinions, and Executive Orders; information on legislative committees and schedules; information on legislators; and links to the House and the Senate websites.

Office of the State Register, http://doa.louisiana.gov/osr/osr.htm

Featured Information: the *Louisiana Administrative Code*, the *Louisiana Register*, and executive orders. The Office of the State Register is charged with publishing all administrative documents emanating from the governor and from executive agencies, boards, and commissions.

The Official Website of the State of Louisiana, http://louisiana.gov

Featured Information: all things Louisiana, including extensive linking to Louisiana resources from all three branches of government and information necessary to a lawyer who has clients doing business in the state. The *Service*, *Business*, and *Government* icons on the website provide information including an index of Louisiana state agencies; an index of Louisiana boards and commissions; a federal government section with links to federal government websites; links to other states' web portals; and a link to search municipal codes from within the state.

Louisiana State Bar Association, www.lsba.org

Featured Information: extensive links to law-related websites, Louisiana court websites, and Louisiana government websites; information on the structure of the court system, with a description of the courts and their jurisdiction; information on the Louisiana Attorney Disciplinary Board and disciplinary procedures; judicial interest rate and judicial interest rate calculator; information on CLE requirements and offerings; Louisiana Rules of Professional Conduct; and Louisiana Rules of Professionalism.

Louisiana State Law Institute, www.lsli.org

Featured Information: information on the purpose of the Institute; a list of Institute committees; biennial report; and recent legislation proposed by the Institute.

II. Websites Focusing on Federal Law

United States Government Printing Office, www.gpo.gov

Featured Information: allows access to documents and laws from the three federal branches of government; searchable databases for a wide variety of federal documents; links to federal agency websites and the Supreme Court; and a list of all resources available through the website.

Library of Congress, http://thomas.loc.gov

Featured Information: in-depth information on the United States Congress; searchable databases of bills and resolutions, the United States Code, the Congressional Record, Committee Reports, and treaties.

United States Fifth Circuit Court of Appeals, www.ca5.uscourts.gov

Featured Information: general contact information for the court; court calendar; court rules; Practitioner's Guide to the U.S. Court of Appeals; sample briefs and forms; searchable database that allows searching of Fifth Circuit published opinions from 1992 to the present; search engine for the Fifth Circuit Library; and links to all federal district courts within the Fifth Circuit, which includes all federal courts in Louisiana.

III. General Websites that Provide Searchable Databases

Below is a list of websites that provide links to sources of law and searchable databases. Searches on some of the free websites will lead you back to some of the state and federal websites noted above. Websites that are free to use are marked with an (f), and websites that involve a fee and registration are marked with a dollar sign ($).

Westlaw ($), www.westlaw.com

LexisNexis ($), www.lexisnexis.com

Loislaw ($), www.loislaw.com

Bloomberg Law ($), www.bloomberg.com/solutions/business_solutions/law

VersusLaw ($), www.versuslaw.com

Legal Information Institute of Cornell University Law School (f), www.law.cornell.edu

American Law Sources On-line (f), www.lawsource.com/also

FindLaw for Legal Professionals (f), http://lp.findlaw.com

Casemaker (free to members of some state bar associations), www.casemaker.us

FastCase (free to members of some state bar associations), www.fastcase.com

Google Scholar (f), http://scholar.google.com

Social Science Research Network (f), www.ssrn.com/lsn

About the Author

Mary Garvey Algero is the Warren E. Mouledoux Distinguished Professor of Law at Loyola University New Orleans, College of Law, where she directs the Legal Research and Writing program and teaches courses in research and writing, civil procedure, and ethics. Prior to teaching, she practiced law in Louisiana. While in law school she served as the editor in chief of the *Loyola Law Review*.

Index